The Best of British Baking

The Best of *British* BAKING

Classic Sweet Treats and Savory Bakes

MARIE RAYNER

Photography by
Darren Muir

ROCKRIDGE
PRESS

For general information on our other products and services or to obtain technical support, please contact our Customer Care Department within the United States at (866) 744-2665, or outside the United States at (510) 253-0500.

Rockridge Press publishes its books in a variety of electronic and print formats. Some content that appears in print may not be available in electronic books, and vice versa.

Interior and Cover Designer: Mando Daniel
Art Producer: Sara Feinstein
Editor: Anne Lowrey
Production Editor: Andrew Yackira
Production Manager: Martin Worthington

Photography © 2021 Darren Muir. Food Styling by Yolanda Muir. Author photo courtesy of Body Confidence Photography.

Hardcover ISBN: 978-1-63878-643-6
Paperback ISBN: 978-1-63807-302-4
eBook ISBN: 978-1-63807-967-5

R0

*For my father, who has always
been my biggest fan*

Contents

Introduction

An exciting thing is happening. In recent years, I've noticed a trend of people wanting to make their own baked goods. Whether they have been inspired by *The Great British Bake Off* or simply want to fill their free time, more people are getting into the kitchen, finding a stand mixer, and grabbing a rolling pin. This is a wonderful thing!

I have always been an avid home baker. When my five children were growing up in Canada, I loved to bake cookies and cakes to put in their packed lunches and offer as afterschool snacks. On weekends I would bake them pies, and of course every holiday or special occasion meant baking even more goodies to help make our family celebrations special. I have never relied on store-baked or processed goods—making my own has always been more rewarding to me.

Yet when I moved to Great Britain to work as a personal chef on a manor estate more than 20 years ago, I had never seen such a wonderful variety of baked goods in my life as what greeted me there. Fruited scones, tiffin bars, Eccles cakes, lemon drizzle cake, sausage rolls, iced buns—there was no end to the tantalizing delights that winked at me from the shop windows!

Cupcakes were not just cupcakes; they were fairy cakes! What in the world is a tiffin cake? How could one fail to fall in love with baked goods with such fancy names? I wanted to try them all, and I really wanted to bake them all. I was inspired by great bakers like Mary Berry and James Martin, who made me believe that I, too, could become a great baker.

Over the next 20 years, my baking journey would take me across the length and breadth of not one but four very individual countries in the United Kingdom: England, Scotland, Wales (which together make up Great Britain), and Northern Ireland (not to be confused with the Republic of Ireland, which is a separate country entirely). Each nation places their own unique stamp and flair on the baked goods produced within their various counties.

Perhaps your ancestors, like some of mine, came to North America from the British Isles. You may have a longing to get back to your roots and taste the cakes and goodies that your grandmother used to bake. Some of you may wish to visit Britain and test out some of their "bakes" and cakes. Maybe you have been inspired by watching British baking shows. Whatever your reasons, your love of British baking has brought you here today to learn more and to "get stuck" into some great British baking recipes, so welcome!

I'm happy to bring to your table all of the expertise and a wealth of knowledge gathered during my years of living and baking in Britain. I promise that new great and tasty things are about to come from your kitchen! Dust off your apron and crack open your baking cupboards. You're about to get started on one of the most delicious baking journeys of your life!

CHAPTER 1

British Baking

When I came to Great Britain, I thought there wouldn't be much difference between the baking I had done at home in Canada and what existed there. This was an English-speaking country, after all. Oh, how wrong I was! Toe-may-toe, toe-*mah*-toe!

British Baking 101

Before working in Great Britain, I had always baked with the most basic ingredients. I had no idea that so many varieties of sugar existed, or even flours. Being so close to the European continent meant that the UK was armed with many more choices for ingredients to use in baking than I'd previously known of.

I found there was a proper way of doing things and a definite regional difference between one area and the next. Since the UK comprises four separate countries, it's not surprising that the cakes and baked goods of each one would vary a great deal!

Generally, I found their baked goods to be less sweet than what I was used to in North America—even the bread. There is a considerable difference.

I soon learned to bake by weight, rather than by volume. Baking by weight is a more accurate way of baking, as it leaves no room for error.

British bakers use more natural ingredients and flavors in their baking and far fewer processed products. They rely heavily on the use of dried fruits and fresh dairy products, of which they have some of the best in the world.

Cake mixes and other baking mixes were not available in Britain when I first arrived. This is a change that has occurred only over the last few years. The British like to bake from scratch!

Once you master the basics through the recipes in this book, there is nothing you won't be able to bake and enjoy. This book contains a multitude of fresh, from-scratch, delicious recipes, varying from simple biscuits (what the British call cookies) to sweet or savory breads and everything in between.

Understanding Culture through Food

Like other cultures throughout the world, British baking has been greatly influenced by the cultural history of each area of Britain, as well as the diversity of products and ingredients grown and produced locally.

One way to really get to know a culture is to dig in to what fuels the people's appetites. There is great cultural diversity in Great Britain, and this reveals itself in many of their dishes, with many hearkening back to the days before colonialism.

You will find that most regions in the United Kingdom are sensitive to the regionality of their baked goods, with many having achieved a Protected Designation of Origin, or PDO, which very much pertains to the region, history, country, and area of its origin. In this book, you will find recipes originating from each country in the UK, and, wherever possible, I have taken great care to highlight their history and origin.

Although England, Scotland, Wales, and Northern Ireland are each a part of the UK, they take great pride in their individuality and have their own separate flower symbols, saints, holidays, traditions, and foods by which they identify themselves. There are also three different languages spoken—English, Welsh, and Gaelic—although the majority of people speak English. Differences stem from the variations in culture and history that each separate country brings to the bountiful table that is Britain. Let it be noted that the English are English, Welsh are Welsh, Scots are Scots, and Irish are Irish. They will be very quick to let you know the difference!

ENGLAND

England is the largest and most populated country in the UK and brings a multiplicity of baked goods to the table. There are many regional differences in baking, with each English county bringing its own unique spin. Baking recipes can vary greatly. Its proximity to "the Continent" (as mainland Europe is lovingly referred to) has also influenced its style of baking.

WALES

Wales, to the west of England, brings an entirely different flavor to the menu, with plenty of griddle or stone cakes (cakes baked on a baking stone), simple fruited breads, seed cakes, and honey cakes. Many Welsh share simple values that are reflected in their style of baked goods; beloved recipes have been handed down from generation to generation with great pride. The Welsh are famous for their delicious Bara Brith (page 77), which is a lovely fruit bread that you will find at every tearoom in the country. It is meant to be enjoyed with plenty of fresh Welsh butter and hot tea.

SCOTLAND

Scotland, to the north of England, is a large and diverse country, with plenty of coastline, beautiful highlands, and myriad inland lakes and rivers. The cuisine of Scotland is quite simple but has also been heavily influenced by the French. Mary, Queen of Scots brought with her many of the traditions and flavors of France, having been brought up in the French Court. Scotland also grows some of the finest raspberries and oats to be found in the world. You may not find much in the way of fancy iced buns or cakes heavily laden with buttercream icing coming from their bake shops, but you will find some of the best shortbread biscuits and oat cakes on the planet.

NORTHERN IRELAND

The Irish and Northern Irish diet has long relied heavily on potatoes, and so potatoes show up at most meals, often more than once. Irish potato farls are common breakfast breads, made from leftover potatoes, traditionally baked on a stone griddle or "girdle," and best enjoyed alongside an Ulster Fry. Speaking of bread, nothing can compete with a slice of warm Irish soda bread slathered with fresh Irish butter (try the widely available Kerrygold or Northern Irish brand, Abernethy butter), produced by cows fed on that beautiful green grass.

A Brief Trip through (Baking) History

History has played a large part in the development of baking and baked goods in Great Britain. Many other cultures and peoples have greatly influenced British baking. The Norse invaders, the Normans, the Celts, and the Romans all left their marks on British culture and British baking, with lots of traditional dishes from their homelands adapted to what was grown and available for use in Great Britain. This influence has created a food culture that is diverse and quite unique.

British Baking versus North American Baking

One thing that all four countries in the UK have in common is their use of wholesome and natural ingredients. You will find that their cakes are not as sweet as North American cakes, nor are their biscuits (cookies). They rely a lot on dried and candied fruit and have long benefited from having been a seafaring region with easy access to goods, nuts, and spices from all over the world.

The British love their puddings, and by that I don't mean what North Americans usually understand pudding to be. *Pudding* is a term the British use to describe the dessert course of the meal, not a milky concoction to be eaten with a spoon. To the British, pudding includes a wide variety of cakes, "bakes" (baked goods), and pies.

You will find their cakes and bakes to be quite simple in comparison to those found in North America. If there is frosting at all, it will likely be a glacé, which is more like a glaze. Most cakes are topped only with a dusting of sugar. Jam figures hugely in their bakes and is often used to fill cakes, cookies, and tarts. Raspberry jam is most commonly used, but the British are also fond of marmalade cakes and use apricot jam to glaze many baked goods. Buttercream icings are used to fill and top cakes, such as a coffee and walnut cake.

The Hallmarks of British Baking

Many British desserts are accompanied by jugs of warm custard, which they love to pour over their desserts, be it a lush chocolate gateau or a warm apple crumble. They also enjoy lashings of heavy unsweetened cream poured over the top.

Biscuits in the UK are cookies, and most of them are meant to be dunked in and washed down with hot cups of tea. Flapjacks are not pancakes but chewy oat bars, sometimes filled with nuts and dried fruits, and often topped with chocolate.

British flour for the most part is unbleached and comes in different weights, each meant for different uses. They also have a wide variety of sugars and mainly use butter in their baking. Shortening is not used on a regular basis, although you will sometimes see margarine being called for (but not in this book).

Dried and candied fruits are used far more often than chocolate. When chocolate is used, the British like to use good chocolate with a high cacao count. Sweetened shredded coconut is not to be found at all; it is always desiccated, which is much smaller and drier, and comes both sweetened and unsweetened. Larger shaved pieces of coconut make fabulous decorations for cakes and confections. Ginger is another favorite flavor here. You might see four different kinds being used in one bake: ground, candied, preserved, and fresh!

There are five common kinds of pastry: short crust, rough puff, puff, choux, and hot water. There are variations on these as well. Cakes tend to be dense and buttery, and there is no end to the types of pies on offer, both sweet and savory.

Baking Staples

The following ingredients are the ones you will find used in this book. I have highlighted some ingredients that you may not be familiar with. Wherever possible, I explain their uses and where you can find them. Ingredients suggested for each recipe are the best ones to use for that recipe; proper results cannot be guaranteed otherwise. I also offer suitable substitutions where I can.

Flours

Several flours are available in Britain, each lending its own property to the bake. It is important to use the right kind of flour for each recipe, as to do otherwise can greatly affect the outcome.

All-purpose (also known as plain) flour: This flour is generally used for cakes, biscuits, pastries, or any recipe requiring a flour with a low gluten content. This type of flour is used most in the recipes in this book.

Bread flour: Commonly called strong flour in the UK, this flour has a higher gluten content and is thus best suited for making breads.

Self-rising flour: This is an all-purpose flour with a raising agent added to it. Commonly used for baking cakes in the UK as well as scones, self-rising flour is not always easy to find, so I've included instructions on how to make your own (see page 22).

Whole-wheat flour: This flour has not had the bran or germ removed from it. It comes in both plain and self-rising varieties, and is known as whole-meal flour in the UK.

Cornstarch: This is commonly known as corn flour in the UK.

Sugars

Many bakers choose to use unrefined or less refined sugars in their bakes. There is a subtle difference in flavor, but overall you will have just as much success if you have access to only more refined sugars.

Caster sugar: This sugar is the one most used for baking. With a finer texture than regular granulated sugar, it blends smoothly, producing baked goods with a more even texture. If you are unable to find caster sugar, you can process regular granulated sugar in a food processor to give you finer granules.

Icing sugar: Also known as confectioners' sugar or powdered sugar, this very fine sugar is used for making icings and glazes and for dusting over finished baked goods.

Brown sugar: This comes in both light and dark varieties. It is the same as North American light and dark brown sugar but is referred to in the UK as being soft, so you'll see it in recipes as "soft (light or dark) brown sugar." I think the term *soft* is there because it has a higher moisture content than granulated sugar and is not free-flowing. This is largely due to the inclusion of molasses. The more molasses in the sugar, the browner it will be.

Demerara sugar: This is a less refined sugar than regular granulated sugar. Also known as turbinado sugar, demerara has a much coarser grain and darker color, although not as dark as brown sugar. It is mainly used for dusting the tops of cakes and bakes for a crunchy texture.

Golden syrup, dark treacle, and honey: Golden syrup is unique to the UK. It can be difficult to find in North America except in specialty shops or online. It has an almost caramel-like flavor, with lemon undertones. Golden Eagle Syrup is a suitable substitute. Dark treacle is like molasses but with a somewhat stronger flavor. You can use molasses in its place, although it may not give you quite the same kick as dark treacle. Alternatively, you can purchase it online. Honey is nature's sweetener. It is suggested that you use clear, runny honey, as it dissolves much easier than the creamed variety.

Leaveners

A leavener is something added to a baked good to give it lift or to make it rise. There are only three leaveners used in the recipes in this book, all of which are common and easy to find.

Baking powder

Baking soda

Yeast: I call for fast-acting or regular dried yeast, depending on the recipe.

Fats

Fats add richness, moisture, and flavor to baked goods. Baked goods with added fat taste better and feel better in the mouth. They also have a much nicer texture.

Butter: European butter tends to be less salty and lighter in color than North American butter. If you are able to source European butter, I recommend using it. If you cannot find European butter and need to use North American butter, use a lightly salted variety—or use unsalted butter and add salt as needed to the recipe.

Lard: Lard is a pork fat that has no discernible taste. It works beautifully in pastries. It has a higher melting point than butter or shortening and produces a delectable, flaky result.

Suet: Suet is the hard white fat found on the kidneys and loins of animals, predominantly sheep and cattle. It is a crumbly fat used to make foods such as puddings, pastries, and mincemeat filling. You can find it in specialty shops or online. In a pinch, you can use frozen grated butter or shortening instead, although the finished product may have a slightly different flavor.

Spices and Flavorings

All the spices and flavorings used in this book are fairly simple. For that reason, I highly recommend that you use the freshest and purest spices and flavorings you can access.

Ground cinnamon

Ground ginger

Whole nutmeg: I prefer to grate my own, as it has a much fresher flavor.

Mixed spice: This is a specialty baking spice, similar to pumpkin or apple pie spice. The British use it a lot in their baking. You can easily make your own, which I recommend. Just mix together 1 tablespoon ground cinnamon, 1 teaspoon each ground coriander and ground or grated nutmeg, ½ teaspoon ground ginger, and ¼ teaspoon each ground cloves and ground allspice. Store in an airtight container, out of the light, for up to 6 months.

Pure vanilla extract

Dairy Products and Eggs

Butter: I recommend using European butter, or else lightly salted or unsalted North American butter.

Cream: In the UK we have double cream (equivalent to heavy whipping cream in the US) and single cream (for which you can use half-and-half).

Eggs: All eggs used are large free-range eggs, unless otherwise indicated.

Milk: I use homogenized whole milk.

Add-Ins

These ingredients will be required in some recipes for complete authenticity.

Apricot and raspberry jams

Blanched whole almonds

Candied citrus peel: This can be purchased online and in British supply shops. You can also find it in some grocery stores in the baking section. A recipe for making your own is on page 76.

Candied ginger: This is available online or at specialty shops.

Custard powder: Bird's is the most common brand and can be purchased in some well-stocked grocery stores, British supply shops, or online.

Dried pitted dates

Dried raisins, currants, and sultanas (golden raisins)

Flaked (very thinly sliced) almonds

Glacé cherries: These can be found in the baking section of some grocery stores. If you cannot find them, you can use rinsed and dried maraschino cherries.

Ground almonds: This is often labeled almond meal or almond flour.

Marzipan: This thick almond paste is used to wrap or fill cakes.

Old-fashioned or rolled oats

Walnut halves

How to Select the Proper Tea

What is a good bake without tea? The British love to pair a fresh biscuit or slice of cake with a nice hot cup of tea. It is commonly thought that hot tea can solve all of life's problems. Tea was not actually introduced into Britain until the 1700s, but once it was, it proved to be so popular that the British are now the largest consumers of tea in the world. Once a luxury reserved only for the upper classes, it is now quite affordable for all.

For everyday use, I would recommend a good orange pekoe tea. An English or Irish breakfast tea will serve you very well from morning to midafternoon. Reserve specialty teas such as Earl Grey for occasions such as tea parties, or in the late afternoon for a special pick-me-up.

"High tea," or afternoon teatime, is a bit of a small meal, involving finger sandwiches, small savories such as sausage rolls, and something sweet like a slice of cake, cookie, or tart. It is meant to stave off hunger until dinnertime, which can sometimes be as late as 8:00 or 9:00 p.m. A typical teatime menu using some of the recipes from this book might include Sausage Rolls (page 82), Classic Fruited Scones (page 42) with cream and jam, and a slice of Victoria Sponge Cake (page 60).

In other parts of England, suppertime is also known as teatime, a term merely used to signify the evening meal, which is usually served around 6:00 p.m.

Essential Equipment

You will not need much in the way of complicated or unusual equipment to make most recipes in this book. All baking dishes are metal, unless otherwise specified. Metal pans are more proficient heat conductors and cool down more quickly than glass bakeware. They also cook things more evenly.

Baking scale: Although you can certainly bake using standard measuring cups, baking by weight will give you much more accurate results. There are many good digital scales available that will allow you to measure by weight. Most will allow you to add one ingredient, reset the tare, add the next, and so on.

Measuring cups: These are used to measure dry ingredients; they are usually metal with a handle.

Glass measuring cup: This is used to measure liquid ingredients; Pyrex is the best-known brand.

Measuring spoons: You'll need at least 1 tablespoon, 1 teaspoon, ½ teaspoon, and ¼ teaspoon, although other in-between sizes come in handy.

Wooden spoons

Balloon whisks (large and small)

Silicone spatula

Metal spatula

Round metal cookie cutters in a variety of sizes

Rolling pin

Pastry bag with a variety of tips

Pastry brush

Fine wire sieve: This is useful for sifting ingredients together as well as for dusting icing sugar on top of finished baked goods.

Electric hand mixer

Mixing bowls (small, medium, and large): I recommend glass bowls, which can also be used in the microwave.

Rimmed Swiss roll pan (9-by-13-inch)

Large rimmed baking sheets (18-by-26-inch)

Round cake tins: You'll want two 7-inch and two 8-inch pans; I like the kind with removable bottoms.

Rectangular baking tin (7-by-11-inch)

Deep round cake tin or springform pan (9-inch)

Round pie tin (9-inch)

Round tart tin (9-inch)

Shallow tart tin with 12 cups or 12 individual tart tins

Loaf tin (8-by-4-inch)

Square cake tin (7-inch)

Flat griddle pan or large heavy-bottomed nonstick skillet

Wire cooling racks

Helpful But Not Entirely Necessary

Bench scraper

Citrus juicer

Citrus zester

Metal skewer (for testing cakes)

Nutmeg grater or Microplane

Pastry blender (you can use your fingertips or a fork in most cases)

Stand mixer

Using a Digital Scale

A digital scale is a must in my kitchen. It is invaluable for measuring the smallest to the largest of ingredients. There are some great battery-operated ones now, and options to suit every budget.

Measuring by weight is a much more accurate way of baking, as it leaves no room for error. Although both weight and volume measurements are included with the recipes in this book, you will find that measuring by weight is much easier and quicker, as well as more accurate and precise than by volume. Surprisingly, measuring cups can vary a great deal in size, whereas weight never changes.

If using traditional volume measurements, the proper way to measure dry ingredients is to spoon them into a dry measuring cup, without packing them down, and then level them off using the straight side of a knife. One exception to this method is brown sugar, which in most cases is packed into the cup. With brown sugar, if you can dump it out and it holds its shape, you know you have measured correctly. For wet measurements, use dedicated wet measuring cups, which are generally made of glass and have a pouring spout.

Techniques and Tips

There is a right way and a wrong way to do everything in this world, and that includes baking. It is extremely important to do things the right way for positive and consistent results. Following my tips and techniques can help ensure success every time you bake.

Leavening

Make sure that your yeast, baking powder, and baking soda are well within the use-by date as printed on the package.

There are several kinds of yeast available, including fast-acting yeast, which only needs to be mixed into the flour, and regular dried yeast, which must be proofed first. To proof regular dried yeast, follow the directions on the package.

To test the freshness of your baking powder or soda, add some to water. If it bubbles, it is good to go. Normally, when using baking soda in a recipe, you will need to add something acidic to get a good rise. That is why most soda breads also use buttermilk or sour milk.

Preparing Yeast Bread Dough

Kneading is one of the most important parts of making yeast breads. Kneading helps develop the gluten in the bread, enabling it to rise properly. Do not stint on the time required. A properly kneaded dough should be smooth and elastic without any lumps or dry spots. At this point the dough is usually left to rise until doubled in volume.

Next comes shaping. The proper way to shape a traditional yeast loaf is to tip the dough out onto a lightly floured board or countertop. Using a lightly floured rolling pin, press the dough out into a rectangle. Use only enough flour to keep it from sticking. Roll it up tightly from the long edge, pressing the seam shut on the underside. Next, bring each end of the loaf over to the underside, and pinch the seams closed. You can then place your loaf into the tin or onto the baking sheet, seam-side down and leave it to rise again.

This second rising is (perhaps confusingly) also referred to as proofing. Underproofed or overproofed yeast doughs will not rise properly in baking. To test if your dough is proofed enough, poke your index finger into it. If it springs back right away, the dough needs to rise for a bit longer. If your finger leaves an indentation that springs back slowly, then the dough has proofed enough. If you have overproofed your dough, it will not spring back at all. This means that most of the air bubbles in your dough have collapsed—but not to worry, you can still rescue it. Simply punch down your dough again, reshape, and allow it to proof again.

Mixing Batter

For ideal cakes, it is recommended that all ingredients come to room temperature before beginning, unless specified otherwise. Unsurprisingly, beating by hand will take longer than if beating with an electric mixer. Generally, cake batters should be beaten only long enough for all the ingredients to be combined thoroughly, with no dry streaks or lumps remaining. Overmixing results in a cake that does not rise as tall, with a tough crumb.

For quick breads, it is acceptable to have a few lumps in the mix. For best results, mix only to just combine.

Cutting Butter into Flour

With scones, the fat is rubbed into the flour using your fingertips with a snapping motion. It is important to work quickly so the fat does not melt. As you are rubbing, lift your flour up into air. This helps aerate the flour and gives a nicer rise. Be careful not to overwork your dough. A light touch is your best tool.

With pastry, it is important to keep everything cold so the fat is incorporated into the flour rather than melted into the flour. Cut in the fat using a pastry blender, using an up-and-down motion with a slight twist. Ideally your flour-fat mixture should contain pea-size clumps of fat. If you overhandle the dough, you will have a tough pastry. Keep a small amount of the flour in reserve for when you are rolling it out, so you don't add too much extra flour into the mix, which can result in a drier, tougher pastry.

Rolling Out and Shaping Dough

A light touch is best when working with dough that needs to be rolled or patted out. Resist the urge to over-flour your countertop, rolling pin, or hands. When making scones, try to get as many scones cut from the first cut. Scones made from the scraps and re-rolls will not be as tender. Take care not to stretch your pastry as you are fitting it into a pie tin, as stretched pastry shrinks.

Knowing When Your Bake Is Done

Bread: It should be golden brown on top and sound slightly hollow when tapped on the underside.

Cake: The top should spring back when lightly touched. A toothpick inserted into the center should come out clean.

Cookies: They should look firm and be lightly browned on the bottoms and just around the edges. A finger poke should not leave an indentation.

Pastries: They should be dry, golden brown, and flaky-looking, never doughy or pale.

Pies: The outer ring of the filling in single-crust pies should be firm, with only a slight jiggle in the center. This will firm up as the pie cools. For double-crust pies, the upper crust should be flaky and golden brown, with the filling bubbling up through any air vents. The filling in a meat pie should register 160°F on a probe thermometer.

Where to Begin

Each chapter in this book contains simple, delicious, classic bakes that are guaranteed to get you into the kitchen baking. With handy tips, you can be sure to get the best out of each recipe. Looking for a crisp oat-filled buttery hobnob to dunk into hot tea? You can find this recipe on page 28. Do you enjoy a light flaky scone studded with fruit? Try the Classic Fruited Scone on page 42. Fancy a simple cake to help celebrate a special occasion or just because? Try the lush Victoria Sponge Cake on page 60.

Want a flaky yet savory bake? Perhaps my Sausage Rolls recipe on page 82 will suit you! Can you picture yourself cozying up to a cup of tea and a toasted crumpet in front of the fire this winter? I can! Find my tasty recipe on page 116. I assure you, they are a lot easier to bake than you might think!

Handy Recipe Tips

Ingredient Tips: Additional information on selecting and buying ingredients and working with them.

Technique Tips: Tips for prepping, assembling, and baking more efficiently and successfully.

Variation Tips: Suggestions for adding or changing ingredients to mix things up or try something new with the recipe. Boring stops here!

Now that you are armed to the hilt with everything you need to know, it's time to put on your "pinny" and get into the kitchen. Let the baking begin!

CHAPTER 2

Biscuits and Shortbreads

Viennese Whirls, 22

Digestive Biscuits

I can almost guarantee that you will find a packet of these in the cupboard of every kitchen in the UK. Crisp, buttery, and delicious, they are one of Britain's most popular biscuits, perfect for dunking into a hot cup of tea. *Makes 24*

PREP TIME: 15 minutes **BAKE TIME:** 15 minutes

⅔ cup (100 grams)
  whole-wheat flour

¼ cup (35 grams)
  all-purpose flour, plus
  more for dusting

1 tablespoon rolled oats
  (not old-fashioned oats)

½ teaspoon
  baking powder

8 tablespoons
  (1 stick/110 grams)
  butter, softened

½ cup (100 grams)
  soft light brown
  sugar, packed

1 to 4 tablespoons
  whole milk

1. Preheat the oven to 375°F/190°C. Line two rimmed baking sheets with parchment paper and set aside.

2. In a bowl, whisk the whole-wheat and all-purpose flours with the oats and baking powder. Set aside.

3. In another bowl, cream the butter and brown sugar by hand until light and fluffy. Stir in the flour and oat mixture and combine well. Begin adding the milk, 1 tablespoon at a time. Add only enough milk to give you a thick dough, suitable for rolling. The dough should not be tacky or crumbly.

4. Tip the dough out onto a lightly floured surface and knead it gently until you have a smooth ball. Try not to overhandle the dough.

5. Using a lightly floured rolling pin, roll the dough out to ⅛ inch thickness. Cut into rounds using a 3-inch cookie cutter. Use a spatula to transfer to the prepared baking sheets. Repeat until all of the dough has been used, reworking and cutting any scraps. Prick each cookie once or twice with the tines of a fork.

6. Bake for 15 minutes, until crisp and golden brown around the edges. Transfer to wire racks to cool completely. Store in an airtight container.

Technique Tip: Try to get as many cookies as you can from the first cuts. Reworked scraps will not be quite as nice as first cuts.

Variation Tip: Baked and cooled cookies can be dipped in melted chocolate for an extra special treat. Melt some semisweet or milk chocolate chips in the microwave according to package directions. Spread a small amount of melted chocolate on top of each cookie with a small offset spatula.

Viennese Whirls

These beautiful, buttery cookies literally melt in your mouth. They are sometimes sandwiched together in pairs around vanilla buttercream icing. I prefer them adorned with a small piece of glacé cherry. Don't skip the chill time—it's essential for best results. *Makes 20*

PREP TIME: 15 minutes, plus 30 minutes to chill **BAKE TIME:** 15 minutes

1 cup (2 sticks/225 grams) butter

⅔ cup (75 grams) icing (confectioners') sugar, sifted

1⅔ cups (225 grams) self-rising flour (see tip)

⅛ teaspoon vanilla extract

5 red glacé cherries, washed, dried, and quartered

1. Line a rimmed baking sheet with parchment paper and set aside.

2. Using an electric hand mixer, cream the butter and sugar together until well combined and very soft. If not creamed enough, your dough will be too stiff to pipe. Stir in the flour and vanilla.

3. Transfer the dough to a piping bag fitted with a large star nozzle. Pipe the dough into rosettes on the prepared baking sheet, at least 2 inches apart. Place a piece of cherry on top of each.

4. Place the baking sheet in the refrigerator to chill for 30 minutes.

5. Preheat the oven to 350°F/180°C.

6. Bake the chilled cookies for 15 minutes, until firm and just beginning to turn golden around the edges. Transfer to a wire rack to cool completely. Store in an airtight container.

Ingredient Tip: You can easily make your own self-rising flour. Simply add 1½ teaspoons baking powder and ½ teaspoon salt to every 1 cup (140 grams) all-purpose flour needed.

Melting Moments

These crisp cookies have a lovely, almost shortbread-like texture. Rolled in oats and topped with a tiny piece of a glacé cherry, they are wonderful enjoyed with a hot cup of tea. *Makes 16 to 20*

PREP TIME: 15 minutes **BAKE TIME:** 15 to 20 minutes

½ cup (40 grams) rolled oats (not old-fashioned oats)

3 tablespoons butter, softened

5 tablespoons (69 grams) lard

6 tablespoons (72 grams) fine granulated sugar (caster sugar)

1 large free-range egg yolk, slightly beaten

⅛ teaspoon vanilla extract

1 cup plus 1½ tablespoons (150 grams) self-rising flour (see tip on page 22)

4 or 5 glacé cherries, washed, dried, and quartered

1. Preheat the oven to 350°F/180°C. Line a rimmed baking sheet with parchment paper and set aside.

2. Put the oats in a bowl and set aside.

3. In a separate bowl, cream the butter, lard, and sugar together until light and fluffy. Beat in the egg yolk and vanilla.

4. Using a wooden spoon, stir in the flour and incorporate thoroughly. (You may need to use your hands to get in the last bits.)

5. Using your hands, roll the dough into 1-inch balls, then roll each ball in the oats to coat.

6. Place the oat-coated balls on the prepared baking sheet, 2 inches apart. Use your thumb to slightly flatten each ball, and place a piece of cherry in the center of each.

7. Bake for 15 to 20 minutes, until light golden brown. Let cool on the baking sheet for several minutes before transferring to a wire rack to cool completely. Store in an airtight container.

Custard Creams

These crisp biscuits have a beautiful crumbly texture and are sandwiched with a delicious custard-flavored buttercream filling. A food processor is very helpful to make these. You can also make them with an electric mixer, but it will take longer to bring the dough together. *Makes 24*

PREP TIME: 15 minutes, plus 20 minutes to chill **BAKE TIME:** 10 minutes

For the cookies

1⅔ cups (225 grams) all-purpose flour, plus more for dusting

⅓ cup (52 grams) custard powder

¼ cup (30 grams) icing (confectioners') sugar, sifted

¾ cup (1½ sticks/170 grams) butter, diced

½ teaspoon vanilla extract

For the filling

3½ tablespoons butter, softened

1½ cups (200 grams) icing (confectioners') sugar, sifted

2 tablespoons custard powder

1 to 2 tablespoons whole milk (if needed)

To make the cookies

1. Combine the flour, custard powder, and icing sugar in the bowl of a food processor. Pulse to combine.

2. Drop in the diced butter and vanilla. Pulse just until everything begins to come together (12 to 15 pulses). (Alternatively, you can combine all the cookie ingredients in a bowl and beat with an electric mixer until everything comes together.)

3. Tip the dough out onto a large piece of plastic wrap. Bring the dough together into a smooth, flat disk and wrap tightly. Place in the refrigerator to chill for 10 minutes.

4. Line two rimmed baking sheets with parchment paper. Using a lightly floured rolling pin, roll the chilled dough out to ¼ inch thickness. Cut into rounds using a 2-inch cookie cutter. Place on the prepared baking sheets and prick the tops with a fork. Place back in the refrigerator to chill for another 10 minutes.

5. Preheat the oven to 350°F/180°C. Bake the chilled cookies for 10 minutes, just until they begin to color around the edges. Cool on the baking sheets for 5 minutes, then carefully transfer to a wire rack to cool completely.

To make the filling and finish

6. Combine the butter, icing sugar, and custard powder in a bowl and beat with an electric hand mixer until smooth and fluffy. Add a bit of milk if needed, a tablespoon or less at a time, until thick, creamy, and spreadable.

7. Sandwich the cooled cookies together with the buttercream. Store in an airtight container.

Chocolate Bourbon Biscuits

These sugar-dusted rich chocolate biscuits boast a wonderful creamy filling. Contrary to the name, they do not actually contain any bourbon. Traditionally, each individual cookie has 10 holes poked into it with the flat end of a wooden skewer. *Makes 14*

PREP TIME: 15 minutes **BAKE TIME:** 10 minutes

For the cookies
3½ tablespoons butter
¼ cup (50 grams) soft light brown sugar, packed
1 tablespoon golden syrup
¾ cup (105 grams) all-purpose flour, plus more for dusting

3 tablespoons unsweetened cocoa powder, sifted
½ teaspoon baking soda
1 to 2 teaspoons whole milk
2 tablespoons granulated sugar, for sprinkling

For the filling
3½ tablespoons butter, softened
1 cup (130 grams) icing (confectioners') sugar, sifted
1 tablespoon unsweetened cocoa powder
2 teaspoons whole milk
⅛ teaspoon vanilla extract

To make the cookies

1. Preheat the oven to 300°F/150°C. Line a rimmed baking sheet with parchment paper and set aside.

2. In a bowl, cream the butter and brown sugar together with an electric hand mixer until light and fluffy. Beat in the golden syrup until well combined.

3. In another bowl, whisk together the flour, cocoa powder, and baking soda. Sift this mixture into the creamed mixture. Add the milk, a little at a time, until soft, even, and a bit crumbly.

4. Tip the dough out onto a lightly floured surface. Knead gently until the dough comes together completely, about a minute. Using a lightly floured rolling pin, roll the dough out to an 8-by-12-inch rectangle roughly ¼ inch thick. Cut into 14 rectangles, about 1¼ inches by 2¾ inches.

5. Using the flat end of a skewer, punch 10 indents into each rectangle, 5 along each long edge. Do not punch all the way through. Dust the cookies with the granulated sugar. Carefully transfer to the prepared baking sheet using a spatula.

6. Bake for 8 to 10 minutes, until crisp around the edges. Transfer to a wire rack and cool completely.

To make the filling and finish

7. Beat all the filling ingredients together in a bowl using an electric hand mixer until smooth, creamy, and evenly colored. Spread a heaping teaspoon onto the unsugared side of half of the cookies and top with the remaining cookies, sugar-side up. Store in an airtight container.

Homemade Hobnobs

Hobnobs are one of Britain's favorite cookies. This from-scratch version is incredibly "moreish," meaning you will not be able to eat just one. They're crisp and very dunkable. You have been warned. *Makes 20*

PREP TIME: 15 minutes **BAKE TIME:** 25 minutes

10 tablespoons (140 grams) butter

¾ cup (140 grams) fine granulated sugar (caster sugar)

1 tablespoon whole milk

1 teaspoon golden syrup

1 teaspoon baking soda

1 cup (140 grams) self-rising flour (see tip on page 22)

1⅓ cups (110 grams) rolled oats (not old-fashioned oats)

1. Preheat the oven to 300°F/150°C. Line a rimmed baking sheet with parchment paper and set aside.

2. In a bowl, cream the butter and sugar together until light and fluffy. Using an electric hand mixer, beat in the milk, golden syrup, and baking soda until well mixed. Stir in the flour and oats by hand, making sure they are well combined.

3. Divide and shape into 20 evenly sized balls, and place them 2 inches apart on the prepared baking sheet.

4. Bake for 25 minutes, until golden brown around the edges and set. Cool on the baking sheet for several minutes before transferring to a wire rack to cool completely. Store in an airtight container.

Variation Tip: These treats are sometimes dipped in chocolate. Melt a quantity of semisweet or milk chocolate in the microwave according to the package directions. Dip the bottoms of the baked and cooled cookies in the melted chocolate and place on a piece of wax paper to sit until the chocolate is completely set.

Gingernuts

These delicious, crunchy biscuits flavored with spice and ginger are the perfect dunkers. They are quick to make and a real all-round family pleaser. *Makes 4 dozen*

PREP TIME: 15 minutes **BAKE TIME:** 15 minutes

2 cups (280 grams) all-purpose flour

1 tablespoon ground ginger

½ teaspoon baking soda

½ teaspoon mixed spice (see page 8)

1 cup (200 grams) soft light brown sugar, packed

½ cup (1 stick/110 grams) cold butter, cut into bits

1 tablespoon golden syrup

¼ cup (60 mL) boiling water

1. Preheat the oven to 350°F/180°C. Line two baking sheets with parchment paper. Set aside.

2. Sift the flour, ginger, baking soda, and mixed spice into a bowl. Stir in the brown sugar. Drop in the butter and rub the mixture together with your fingertips until it resembles fine dry bread crumbs.

3. Stir the golden syrup and boiling water together until the syrup melts. Add this mixture to the flour-butter mixture and stir everything together with a butter knife until the mixture forms a soft dough.

4. Pinch off 2 tablespoons of dough and shape into a ball using the palms of your hands. Place on the prepared baking sheets, leaving 2 inches between each ball. Flatten slightly with your fingertips.

5. Bake for 15 minutes, until golden brown and firm. Cool on the baking sheets for 15 minutes or until well set. Use a metal spatula to transfer to a wire rack to cool completely. Store in an airtight container.

Empire Biscuits

These rich, buttery biscuits are a Scottish teatime classic. They are sandwiched together with raspberry jam, glazed with a sweet icing sugar glaze, and topped with half a glacé cherry. *Makes 20*

PREP TIME: 15 minutes **BAKE TIME:** 15 minutes

1 cup (225 grams) butter, softened

Scant ½ cup (85 grams) fine granulated sugar (caster sugar)

1 large free-range egg, lightly beaten

3 cups (420 grams) all-purpose flour, plus more for dusting

2 cups (260 grams) icing (confectioners') sugar, sifted

4 to 6 tablespoons whole milk

10 glacé cherries, washed, dried, and halved

½ to ⅔ cup raspberry jam, for filling

1. Preheat the oven to 400°F/200°C. Line two baking sheets with parchment paper and set aside.

2. In a large bowl, stir the butter and sugar together with a wooden spoon until well combined and a bit granular, but not creamed. Stir in the egg, mixing it in well, and then quickly rub in the flour using your fingertips in a quick snapping motion until it becomes crumbly.

3. Tip the dough out onto a lightly floured surface and knead it gently until you have a smooth dough.

4. Using a lightly floured rolling pin, roll the dough out to ⅛ inch thickness. Cut into rounds using a 2½-inch cookie cutter. Transfer to the prepared baking sheets using a metal spatula.

5. Bake for 15 to 20 minutes, carefully turning them over halfway through. They will be done when they are just barely colored. Scoop onto wire racks to cool completely.

6. Mix the icing sugar with enough milk to make a thick, spreadable glaze. Spread the glaze over the tops of half of the cooled cookies, then place half a piece of cherry in the middle of each. Allow to set.

7. Spread up to 1½ teaspoons of raspberry jam on the remaining cookies, spreading it completely to the edges. Top each with a glazed cookie, glazed-side up.

Technique Tip: The granulated sugar most used for baking in the UK is caster sugar. It is a fine granulated sugar, noted for its ability to melt into bakes without leaving any grit behind. You can easily create your own if your sugar is particularly coarse by pulsing regular granulated sugar in a food processor.

Millionaire's Shortbread Bars

Thought to be a Scottish recipe, these bars boast a crisp and buttery short-bread crust, with a sweet caramel filling and rich chocolate topping. You'll need a food processor for the shortbread base. This is a decadent and very "moreish" bar—that is, irresistible! *Makes 12*

PREP TIME: 15 minutes, plus 1 hour inactive time **BAKE TIME:** 20 minutes

For the shortbread base
½ cup (1 stick/
110 grams) butter
1¼ cups (175 grams)
all-purpose flour, plus
more for dusting
¼ cup (55 grams) fine
granulated sugar
(caster sugar)

For the caramel filling
¾ cup
(1½ sticks/170 grams)
butter
½ cup plus
1½ tablespoons
(115 grams) fine granu-
lated sugar (caster sugar)
3 tablespoons
golden syrup

1 (14-ounce/400 grams)
can sweetened
condensed milk (not
evaporated milk)

For the topping
8 ounces (200 grams)
semisweet chocolate,
broken into pieces

1. Preheat the oven to 350°F/180°C. Butter a 9-inch square baking tin and line it with parchment paper, leaving some excess overhang for ease in lifting out the finished bars.

To make the shortbread base

2. Combine the butter, flour, and sugar in the bowl of a food processor. Pulse until the mixture begins to bind together, about 10 pulses. Tip the mixture into the prepared baking tin. Using lightly floured fingertips, press the mixture into the tin evenly, smoothing over the top. Bake for 20 to 25 minutes, until completely set and golden brown around the edges.

To make the caramel filling

3. While the base is baking, combine the butter, sugar, golden syrup, and condensed milk in a medium saucepan. Gently heat over low heat, stirring continuously, until the sugar has completely dissolved and is not gritty.

4. Bring the mixture to a boil, then reduce to a slow simmer. Stir continuously for 6 to 8 minutes, until the mixture becomes very thick and caramel-colored. Pour the caramel over the top of the baked shortbread base. Place in the refrigerator until cold, about 30 minutes.

To make the topping

5. Melt the chocolate in a heat-proof bowl set over a pan of simmering water. Do not allow the bottom of the bowl to touch the water. Stir until completely melted. Pour the melted chocolate evenly over the top of the chilled caramel base, smoothing it out to cover. Return to the refrigerator to chill until solid, 30 to 45 minutes. Once solid, cut into 12 bars to serve. Store any leftovers in the refrigerator.

Peppermint Petticoat Tails

These charming biscuits make the perfect addition to an afternoon tea. They are called petticoat tails because the ruffled edge is said to resemble the ruffles in a lady's petticoat. The addition of peppermint extract makes these a bit more special. You can, of course, leave it out if you prefer. You will need a 9-inch fluted tart tin with a removable bottom for this pretty treat. *Makes 8*

PREP TIME: 15 minutes, plus 30 minutes to chill **BAKE TIME:** 25 minutes

1 cup plus 2 tablespoons (2¼ sticks/250 grams) butter, softened

½ cup (95 grams) fine granulated sugar (caster sugar)

½ teaspoon peppermint extract

1⅔ cups (250 grams) all-purpose flour, plus more for dusting

⅔ cup (100 grams) cornstarch (corn flour)

½ teaspoon salt

Icing (confectioners') sugar, for dusting

1. Combine the butter, sugar, and peppermint extract in the bowl of a food processor. Pulse together until pale and creamy. (Alternatively, beat with an electric hand mixer until pale and creamy.)

2. Sift together the flour, cornstarch, and salt in a bowl. Tip this mixture into the food processor or mixer and pulse or beat just until the mixture starts to form small clumps.

3. Tip out the dough onto a lightly floured surface and bring the dough together to form a ball. Use a light touch and try not to overwork the dough.

4. Place the ball of dough in a 9-inch fluted tart tin with a removable bottom. Using floured fingers, press the dough to fill the tin as evenly as you can. Use a light touch and try not to really compress the dough.

5. Use the tines of a fork to mark the dough into 8 even wedges, and place the tin in the refrigerator to chill for 30 minutes.

6. Preheat the oven to 350°F/180°C.

7. Place the tart tin on a rimmed baking sheet and bake for 25 minutes, just until it's beginning to turn golden brown around the edges. Remove from the oven and re-mark the edges of the wedges with a fork while still very warm.

8. Cool completely, dust with icing sugar and break into wedges to serve.

Chocolate Tiffin Bars

Chocolate tiffin bars, or tiffin cake as it is also known, is said to be the favorite dessert of Princes William and Harry. There is no real baking involved. They are a quick and easy make for the family without any heating up of the kitchen. Beloved by children, young and old alike, tiffin bars make for great party fare! *Makes 8*

PREP TIME: 10 minutes, plus 1 hour to chill **BAKE TIME:** 15 minutes

7 tablespoons (95 grams) butter

¼ cup golden syrup (in a pinch you can use corn syrup)

3 tablespoons unsweetened cocoa powder, sifted

2 tablespoons soft light brown sugar, packed

1 cup (150 grams) raisins

2½ cups (225 grams) broken digestive biscuits (or broken graham crackers)

8 ounces (225 grams) milk chocolate, melted

1. Generously butter an 8-inch square baking tin, then line with parchment paper, leaving a bit of an overhang. Butter the parchment paper as well. Set aside.

2. Combine the butter, golden syrup, cocoa powder, and brown sugar in a large saucepan. Melt over medium-low heat, stirring constantly, until the sugar no longer feels gritty and everything is well combined. Stir in the raisins.

3. For the best texture, make sure the crumbled biscuits are a mix of sizes, with some larger bits and smaller bits, along with some crumbs. Stir the crumbles into the butter mixture in the pan, mixing everything together until the biscuit pieces are well coated and the raisins are evenly distributed.

4. Tip this mixture into the prepared baking tin. Press into the pan firmly using the bottom of a metal measuring cup. The mixture should be compact.

5. Pour the melted chocolate evenly over the top of the mixture, spreading with an offset spatula to cover the mixture completely.

6. Place in the refrigerator to chill completely, at least an hour.

7. Once set, lift out and cut into squares to serve. Store any leftovers tightly covered in the refrigerator.

Variation Tip: If you like, you can add candied cherries or dried cherries, dried cranberries, or a mix of these along with raisins to make up the same measure of raisins.

Scottish Shortbread

Is there anything on earth more beautiful or delicious than a crumbly short-bread biscuit? I think not! The Scots are immensely proud of their shortbread and quite rightly so. It is important that your butter be the right consistency. It should be soft enough that you can press your finger into the block, leaving a bit of a dent, but not overly so. *Makes 24 to 30 biscuits or 1 (9-by-13-inch) pan*

PREP TIME: 15 minutes, plus 10 minutes to chill **BAKE TIME:** 45 minutes for a full pan

1¼ cups
  (2½ sticks/280 grams)
  butter, softened
¾ cup (140 grams) fine
  granulated sugar (caster

sugar), plus more for
  sprinkling
2 cups (280 grams)
  all-purpose flour

1 scant cup (140 grams)
  cornstarch (corn flour)
Pinch salt

1. In a bowl cream together the butter and sugar using an electric hand mixer until pale in color.

2. Sift together the flour, cornstarch, and salt into another bowl. Stir the flour mixture into the creamed butter-sugar mixture until thoroughly combined, without overmixing. Tip the mixture into a 9-by-13-inch metal baking dish.

3. Using floured hands or an offset spatula, lightly press the mixture into an even layer. Place in the refrigerator to chill for 10 minutes.

4. Preheat the oven to 300°F/150°C.

5. Bake the chilled shortbread for 45 to 55 minutes, until set but not colored.

6. Remove from the oven and immediately sprinkle the top abundantly with more sugar, and then cut into squares or bars. Leave to cool in the baking dish for at least 10 minutes before transferring to a wire rack to cool completely. Store in an airtight container.

CHAPTER 3

Scones and Buns

Honey-Wheat Scones, 44

Classic Fruited Scones

Classic fruited scones are the scones you will see served in just about every tearoom in the UK. They are buttery, tender, and studded with plenty of sticky sultanas, then traditionally served with clotted cream and strawberry jam. There is much debate about which goes on first, the cream or the jam! This decision depends on where your roots lie, but they are delicious no matter which goes on first! *Makes 10*

PREP TIME: 10 minutes **BAKE TIME:** 10 minutes

2½ cups (350 grams) self-rising flour (see tip on page 22), plus more for dusting

1½ teaspoons baking powder

⅓ cup (75 grams) cold butter, cut into bits

2½ tablespoons fine granulated sugar (caster sugar)

½ cup (75 grams) sultanas

2 large free-range eggs

½ to ⅔ cup (120 to 160 mL) whole milk

Demerara sugar, for sprinkling

1. Preheat the oven to 425°F/220°C. Line a rimmed baking sheet with parchment paper and set aside.

2. Sift the flour and baking powder into a bowl, lifting the sieve high above the bowl to get as much air into the flour as you can. Drop the cold butter into the bowl. Using the tips of your fingers and a snapping motion, rub the butter quickly into the flour until the mixture resembles fine dry bread crumbs. Stir in the sugar and sultanas.

3. Beat the eggs in a small bowl. Remove and set aside 2 tablespoons of beaten eggs. Using a fork, beat ½ cup (120 mL) of milk into the remaining beaten eggs. Add the milk mixture to the flour mixture, stirring together with a butter knife. You should have a soft but slightly tacky dough. Add more of the remaining milk if your mixture is too dry. You don't want a gummy, wet mixture, but you also don't want a dry, crumbly mixture.

4. Tip the dough onto a lightly floured surface and knead it gently a few times before patting it out to a round roughly 1 inch thick.

5. Cut into rounds using a 3-inch cookie cutter. Cut using a direct up-and-down motion, without twisting the cutter. Try to get as many cuts as you can from the first cut. Place the scones on the prepared baking sheet as you go. Gather up any scraps, re-pat, and re-cut, until you have 10 scones.

6. Brush the tops with the reserved beaten eggs and sprinkle with a bit of coarse sugar.

7. Bake for 10 minutes, until well risen and golden brown on the tops and bottoms. Scoop onto a wire rack to cool completely. These are best eaten the same day, but you can store leftovers in an airtight container.

Tips for Baking and Enjoying Perfect Scones

→ Keep your butter well chilled so it rubs into the flour mixture, rather than melting into it.

→ Use a light touch when working with the dough. You'll get a much nicer rise and lighter scone if you avoid overworking the dough.

→ Try to get as many scones from the first cutting that you can. Scones cut from reworked and re-patted dough will not be as tender or rise as tall.

→ Do not twist the cutter when cutting out the scones. A sharp up-and-down motion is best. When you twist the cutter, you seal the dough, so the scones rise lopsided in the oven.

→ When brushing the egg on top of the scones, don't let it drip down the sides of the scones. This will also hamper your rise.

→ Unlike baking powder biscuits, most scones are meant to be eaten at room temperature.

→ Clotted cream and jam are really nice accompaniments to scones, but clotted cream is difficult to find in North America. You can use softly whipped cream in its place.

→ Scones go perfectly with a hot cup of tea!

Honey-Wheat Scones

Traditionally, these delightful whole-meal (whole-wheat) flour scones, made often in Northern Ireland, would be sweetened with a good Irish honey. They are baked as a whole round scored into wedges, and then broken apart to eat. Unlike English scones, these are meant to be enjoyed warm with butter. At one time, they would have been baked on an iron "girdle" (griddle) pan over an open fire. *Makes 8*

PREP TIME: 10 minutes **BAKE TIME:** 20 minutes

¾ cup (105 grams) all-purpose flour

¾ cup (105 grams) whole-wheat flour

2 teaspoons baking powder

Pinch salt

⅓ cup (75 grams) butter, softened, plus more for serving

1 tablespoon soft light brown sugar, packed

4 to 5 tablespoons (60 to 80 mL) whole milk

2 tablespoons honey

1. Preheat the oven to 400°F/200°C. Butter a rimmed baking sheet and set aside.

2. Sift the all-purpose flour into a bowl. Whisk in the whole-wheat flour, baking powder, and salt.

3. Drop in the butter and rub it into the flour mixture with your fingertips using a snapping motion until the mixture resembles fine dry bread crumbs. Stir in the brown sugar.

4. Stir the milk and honey together until the honey has totally dissolved. Remove and set aside a tiny bit for glazing the scones. Add just enough of the milk-honey mixture to the flour-butter mixture to make a soft dough, stirring it in with a butter knife.

5. Tip out the dough onto the prepared baking sheet and gently shape into a 7-inch round. With a sharp knife, lightly score the top into 8 wedges without cutting all the way through to the bottom.

6. Bake for 15 to 20 minutes, until dry and set. Remove from the oven and glaze with the reserved milk-honey mixture. Return to the oven for 5 to 10 more minutes, until golden brown.

7. Remove from the oven and break into wedges. Serve warm, split open, with lashings of soft butter. These are best eaten the same day, but you can store leftovers in an air-tight container.

Cheese and Onion Scones

Tender and flaky, these savory scones are delicious on their own, spread with butter, or served alongside a bowl of hot soup. They also make a delicious addition to a traditional British ploughman's lunch, which usually consists of sliced cold meat, some cheese, a bit of pickle, and some salad. Simple and delicious. *Makes 12*

PREP TIME: 10 minutes **BAKE TIME:** 15 minutes

2½ cups (350 grams) all-purpose flour, plus more for dusting
1 tablespoon baking powder
½ teaspoon salt

¼ teaspoon dry mustard powder
½ cup (1 stick/110 grams) cold butter, cut into bits
1 cup (120 grams) grated extra-sharp cheddar cheese, divided

2 scallions, trimmed and finely chopped
1 large free-range egg
1 cup (240 mL) whole milk

1. Preheat the oven to 400°F/200°C. Line a rimmed baking sheet with parchment paper and set aside.

2. Sift the flour, baking powder, salt, and mustard powder into a large bowl. Drop the butter in and rub it into the flour mixture with your fingertips using a snapping motion, until the mixture resembles coarse bread crumbs.

3. Add ¾ cup (90 grams) of cheese and the scallions and stir to combine.

4. In another bowl, beat together the egg and milk. Pour over the flour mixture and stir it in with a fork until you get a soft, shaggy mixture.

5. Tip out the dough onto a lightly floured surface and knead gently 8 to 10 times, just to bring the dough together. Pat into a round about ¾ inch thick.

6. Cut out rounds using a 2½-inch cookie cutter. Try to get as many rounds from the first cut that you can. Gather the scraps together and re-cut until you have 12 rounds. Place on the prepared baking sheet. Sprinkle the remaining ¼ cup (30 grams) of cheese evenly over the tops of the scones.

7. Bake for 15 minutes, until golden brown. Enjoy warm or at room temperature. These are best eaten the same day, but you can store leftovers in an airtight container.

Traditional Rock Cakes

Rock cakes are a rough-drop type of scone, spooned onto a baking sheet and baked. They are filled with lovely bits of sultanas, raisins, chopped dried cherries, and candied citrus peel. These cakes are lovely served warm with butter. These are also said to be Harry Potter's favorite cakes! *Makes 8 to 10*

PREP TIME: 10 minutes **BAKE TIME:** 15 minutes

2 cups (280 grams) all-purpose flour

2 teaspoons baking powder

½ cup (1 stick/110 grams) cold butter, cut into bits

7 tablespoons (85 grams) soft light brown sugar, packed

9 tablespoons (95 grams) mixed dried fruit

Finely grated zest of 1 lemon

1 large free-range egg

1 to 2 tablespoons whole milk

2 teaspoons demerara sugar, for sprinkling

1. Preheat the oven to 400°F/200°C. Butter a rimmed baking sheet and set aside.

2. Sift the flour and baking powder into a large bowl. Drop in the butter and rub it into the flour using a snapping motion with your fingertips, until the mixture resembles coarse sand. Stir in the sugar, dried fruit, and lemon zest.

3. In another bowl, beat the egg and 1 tablespoon of milk. Stir the egg mixture into the flour mixture, adding the other tablespoon of milk only if needed to make a moist but firm and droppable dough.

4. Drop the dough to make 8 to 10 equal heaps on the prepared baking sheet. Sprinkle with the demerara sugar.

5. Bake for 15 to 20 minutes, turning the pan around halfway through the baking time. When done, the cakes will be well risen, golden brown, and firm. Transfer to a wire rack to cool before eating.

Technique Tip: Wash your citrus before using, even if it is unwaxed. Simply rinse under cold water, brush with a vegetable brush, and then dry.

Fat Rascals

These fruity bakes are thought to have originated in the area between Durham and Yorkshire. This recipe dates back to the 1800s. They are more pastry-like and sturdy than a traditional scone, but equally delicious. They go especially well with a nice hot cup of tea in midafternoon. *Makes 7 to 8*

PREP TIME: 10 minutes **BAKE TIME:** 20 minutes

1⅔ cups (225 grams) all-purpose flour, plus more for dusting
Pinch salt
½ cup (1 stick/110 grams) butter, cut into bits and softened

3½ tablespoons fine granulated sugar (caster sugar), plus more for dusting

⅓ cup (50 grams) dried currants
¼ to ⅓ cup (60 to 80 mL) milk and water mixed together

1. Preheat the oven to 400°F/200°C. Generously butter a rimmed baking sheet and set aside.

2. Sift the flour into a bowl. Stir in the salt. Drop in the bits of butter, and using your fingertips and a snapping motion, rub the butter into the flour until the mixture resembles dry bread crumbs. Stir in the sugar and dried currants.

3. Add enough milk-water mixture to the flour mixture to create a firm dough that is not crumbly, nor wet.

4. Tip out the dough onto a floured surface. Pat or roll into a round about ½ inch thick. Cut into rounds using a 3-inch cookie cutter. Place on the prepared baking sheet, leaving some space between each. Dust the tops with additional sugar.

5. Bake for 20 to 25 minutes, until pale golden brown. Carefully transfer to a wire rack to cool completely before serving. These are best eaten the same day.

Yorkshire Rock Cakes

These tasty bakes fall somewhere between a scone and a bun. In Yorkshire they are called fat rascals, but are completely different from the Fat Rascals recipe on page 49! You will want to enjoy these warm, with a cold glass of milk or a hot drink. If you are feeling especially indulgent, you can split them and spread with some butter. *Makes 6*

PREP TIME: 15 minutes **BAKE TIME:** 15 minutes

1 cup plus 1½ tablespoons (150 grams) all-purpose flour

1 cup plus 1½ tablespoons (150 grams) self-rising flour (see tip on page 22)

1 teaspoon baking powder

Pinch salt

½ cup (1 stick/ 110 grams) cold butter, cut into bits

½ cup (95 grams) fine granulated sugar (caster sugar)

Finely grated zest of 1 medium orange

Finely grated zest of 1 lemon

1 teaspoon mixed spice (see page 8)

1 cup (150 grams) mixed dried fruit (sultanas, raisins, currants, and candied citrus peel)

1 large free-range egg plus 1 additional egg yolk

4 to 5 tablespoons whole milk

1 tablespoon water

6 glacé cherries

18 blanched almonds

1. Preheat the oven to 400°F/200°C. Line a rimmed baking sheet with parchment paper and set aside.

2. Sift both flours into a bowl, along with the baking powder and salt. Drop the cold butter into the bowl and quickly rub it into the flour, using your fingertips and a snapping motion, until it resembles fine dry bread crumbs. Stir in the sugar, orange and lemon zests, mixed spice, and dried fruits.

3. In a small bowl, beat the whole egg with 4 tablespoons of milk. Make a well in the flour mixture and add the egg mixture all at once. Stir in using a butter knife to make a soft dough. If the mixture seems dry, add the remaining tablespoon of milk.

4. Divide the mixture equally into 6 portions and gently shape each into a ball. Place the balls spaced well apart on the prepared baking sheet. Using the palm of your hand, gently flatten each to about ¾ inch thick.

5. In a small bowl, beat the egg yolk with the water. Brush the top of each round with the mixture. Press a cherry down into the center and place 3 almonds decoratively around the cherry.

6. Bake for 15 to 20 minutes, until well risen and golden brown. Leave to rest on the baking sheet for 5 minutes, then transfer to a wire rack to cool a bit more. These are best served warm; however, they can be tightly wrapped and frozen, and gently reheated at a later date.

Scottish Oat Cakes

These oaty cakes are delicious, buttery, and crisp. They are lovely served with crumbled cheese or spread with butter and served with a strong cuppa for breakfast. *Makes 32*

PREP TIME: 20 minutes, plus 45 minutes to chill **BAKE TIME:** 40 minutes

¾ cup (60 grams) old-fashioned oats (not instant oats), divided

1½ cups (210 grams) all-purpose flour

¾ cup (150 grams) soft light brown sugar, packed

¾ teaspoon flaked sea salt, plus more for sprinkling

½ teaspoon freshly ground black pepper

¾ cup (1½ sticks/ 170 grams) butter, cut into small pieces

2 to 4 tablespoons cold water

1. Preheat the oven to 350°F/180°C.

2. Spread ½ cup (45 grams) of oats onto a rimmed baking sheet. Toast the oats in the oven for 8 to 10 minutes, until golden brown. Tip the oats into the bowl of a food processor and pulse until finely ground.

3. Pour the ground oats into a large bowl and add the flour, sugar, salt, and pepper. Combine thoroughly.

4. Drop in the butter and rub it into the flour mixture using your fingertips and a snapping motion, until the mixture resembles coarse meal. Stir in 2 tablespoons of water, and then add the remaining tablespoon of water as needed, a bit at a time, until the mixture forms a soft dough. Shape into a flat rectangle and wrap tightly in plastic wrap. Place in the refrigerator to chill for 45 minutes.

5. Preheat the oven again to 350°F/180°C.

6. Unwrap the rectangle of dough and place it on a sheet of parchment paper. Sprinkle the remaining ¼ cup (15 grams) of oats all over the dough. Place another piece of parchment paper on top. Using a rolling pin, roll the dough out into a rectangle about 10 inches by 12 inches.

7. Cut into 32 rectangles, each about 2½ inches by 1½ inches. Using a spatula, transfer to a rimmed baking sheet, spacing them at least 1 inch apart. Sprinkle with flaked sea salt.

8. Bake for 28 to 30 minutes until golden brown. Transfer to a wire rack to cool completely. Store in an airtight container.

Potato Cakes

These traditional savory cakes are proof that what the Northern Irish manage to bake up with potatoes with is always delicious. They are wonderful whether served for breakfast, tea, or supper. Who knew leftover mash could taste so good? *Makes 6*

PREP TIME: 10 minutes **BAKE TIME:** 15 minutes

6 tablespoons (80 grams) cold mashed potatoes

¾ cup (105 grams) all-purpose flour, plus more for dusting

¼ cup (50 grams) lard

Pinch salt

Whole milk, as needed

Butter, for serving

1. Preheat the oven to 400°F/200°C. Butter a rimmed baking sheet and set aside.

2. Mix the potatoes and flour together in a bowl. Rub in the lard with your fingertips until the mixture resembles coarse meal. Mix in the salt and just enough milk to produce a soft, pliable dough.

3. Tip out the dough onto a floured surface. Roll or pat into a round about ½ inch thick. Cut into rounds using a 2½-inch cutter. Place on the prepared baking sheet.

4. Bake for 15 to 20 minutes, until golden brown. Serve immediately, with plenty of butter for spreading on the warm cakes. These are best eaten on the same day, but leftovers can be stored in an airtight container for up to 2 days.

Ingredient Tip: Resist any urge to swap the lard for another fat. Lard works best for this recipe.

Northern Irish Soda Bread

There's nothing quite as comforting as a slice of warm homemade Irish soda bread or farls fresh from the griddle and slathered with plenty of fresh butter and jam. It is also excellent with soups or stews. Here's the quick and easy recipe that's a mainstay in most Northern Irish homes. *Makes 1 (8-inch round) loaf*

PREP TIME: 15 minutes **BAKE TIME:** 25 minutes

3¼ cups (450 grams) all-purpose flour, plus more for dusting

1 teaspoon salt

1 teaspoon baking powder

1 teaspoon fine granulated sugar (caster sugar) (optional)

1¾ cups (420 mL) buttermilk, divided (you may not need it all)

1. Preheat the oven to 425°F/220°C. Lightly butter a rimmed baking sheet and set aside.

2. Sift the flour, salt, and baking powder into a bowl. Whisk in the sugar, if using. Make a well in the center of the dry ingredients. Pour in 1½ cups (360 mL) of buttermilk. Using your fingers, mix everything together to make a soft but not sticky dough. Add some of the remaining ¼ cup (60 mL) of buttermilk, if necessary.

3. Tip the dough out onto a lightly floured surface and knead lightly a few times. It is important not to over-knead the dough as this will toughen it. A few turns is sufficient. Shape the dough into an 8-inch round.

4. Place on the prepared baking sheet. Using a sharp knife, cut a cross in the top, about ½ inch deep.

5. Bake for 25 to 30 minutes. Test that the loaf is done by turning it over and tapping it on the bottom with your knuckles. It should sound hollow.

6. Place on a wire rack to cool, then cut into slices to serve. Soda bread is best eaten on the same day, but leftovers can be stored in an airtight container for up to 2 days. It can also be wrapped tightly and frozen for up to 3 months.

Victoria Scones

These rich scones are baked in rounds, scored into wedges. The cherries on top make them especially pretty. They earn their name, as they're fit for a queen. *Makes 4*

PREP TIME: 10 minutes **BAKE TIME:** 10 minutes

1⅔ cups (225 grams) self-rising flour (see tip on page 22), plus more for dusting
Pinch salt

¼ cup (50 grams) cold butter, cut into bits
¼ cup (50 grams) fine granulated sugar (caster sugar)

1 large free-range egg
7 tablespoons (100 mL) whole milk
4 glacé cherries, cut into quarters

1. Preheat the oven to 400°F/200°C. Line a rimmed baking sheet with parchment paper and set aside.

2. Sift the flour and salt into a bowl. Drop the butter into the bowl and quickly rub it into the flour using your fingertips and a snapping motion. The mixture will resemble fine dry bread crumbs when done. Stir in the sugar.

3. In another bowl, beat the egg and milk together. Remove and set aside a tiny bit to brush on top of the scones.

4. Add the egg-milk mixture to the flour mixture and stir it in with a butter knife to make a soft dough. Tip out the dough onto a lightly floured surface and knead gently a few times.

5. Cut the dough into 4 equal pieces. Shape each piece into a round, roughly ½ inch thick. Place each round on the prepared baking sheet. Using a sharp knife, score the top of each round into 4 sections, without cutting all the way down through the rounds. Brush the reserved egg-milk mixture on top of each scone, and lightly push a piece of cherry into the center of each quarter.

6. Bake for 10 to 15 minutes, until well risen and golden brown. Transfer to a wire rack to cool. Enjoy at room temperature with some butter and jam. These are best eaten the same day, but you can store leftovers in an airtight container.

CHAPTER 4

Cakes and Loaves

Battenberg Cake, 64

Victoria Sponge Cake

Historically, it is said that this cake was originally prepared by one of Queen Victoria's chefs for her birthday. It caught on with the public and has been a popular cake ever since. It makes a great centerpiece for the tea table and is quite simply delicious. *Makes 1 (7-inch) cake*

PREP TIME: 10 minutes **BAKE TIME:** 25 minutes

¾ cup (1½ sticks/170 grams) butter, softened

¾ cup plus 2 tablespoons (170 grams) fine granulated sugar (caster sugar)

¼ teaspoon vanilla extract

3 large free-range eggs, lightly beaten

1¼ cups (170 grams) self-rising flour (see tip on page 22)

3 tablespoons raspberry jam

Icing (confectioners') sugar or additional fine granulated sugar (caster sugar), for dusting

1. Preheat the oven to 350°F/180°C. Generously butter two 7-inch layer cake tins, line the base with parchment paper, and set aside.

2. Using an electric hand mixer or a stand mixer, cream the butter, sugar, and vanilla until fluffy and light in color. Beat in the eggs a bit at a time, beating well with each addition. If the mixture starts to curdle and split, add a tablespoon of the flour mixture.

3. Using a metal spoon, fold in the flour. Use a cutting motion and try not to knock too much of the air out of the mixture. Divide the batter evenly between the prepared baking tins. Level off the surface of each cake and then make a slight dip in the centers using the back of a metal spoon.

4. Bake in the center of the oven for about 25 minutes. The cakes should be well risen and golden brown and should spring back when lightly touched near the center. A toothpick inserted in the center should come out clean.

5. Cool in the pan for 5 minutes. Run a knife around the edge of each cake and then carefully tip out the cake onto a wire rack, gently pulling off the paper. Cool completely.

6. Place one cooled cake layer onto a serving plate, bottom-side up. Spread with the jam, all the way to the edges. Top with the other layer, right-side up. Dust with icing sugar or caster sugar to finish. This will keep for up to 4 days tightly covered.

Variation Tip: You can add a layer of vanilla buttercream icing to the center of the cake along with the jam. To make a simple buttercream, using an electric hand mixer, beat together ¼ cup (50 grams) softened butter, 1 cup (130 grams) sifted icing (confectioners') sugar, and 1 tablespoon whole milk until thick and creamy. Spread over the bottom layer and then top with the jam. Finish as directed.

Coffee and Walnut Cake

This is one of my all-time favorite cakes. With its moist coffee-flavored sponge and coffee buttercream icing, it always pleases. As a bonus, it is an amazingly easy cake to make. *Makes 1 (8-by-4-inch) loaf cake*

PREP TIME: 15 minutes, plus 1 hour to cool **BAKE TIME:** 45 minutes

For the cake
½ cup (120 mL) milk
⅓ cup (75 grams) butter, cut into bits
1 tablespoon instant coffee granules
½ cup (95 grams) fine granulated sugar (caster sugar)

½ cup (60 grams) chopped toasted walnuts, plus toasted walnut halves, for decoration
1 large free-range egg, lightly beaten
1 cup (140 grams) self-rising flour (see tip on page 22), sifted

For the coffee buttercream icing
Scant ½ cup (100 grams) butter, softened slightly
1⅓ cups (160 grams) icing (confectioners') sugar, sifted
1 teaspoon instant coffee, dissolved in 1 teaspoon boiling water
1 to 3 teaspoons whole milk, as needed

To make the cake

1. Preheat the oven to 325°F/160°C. Generously butter an 8-by-4-inch loaf tin and line with baking parchment, leaving an overhang for lifting out the finished cake when done. Set aside.

2. Combine the milk, butter, and coffee granules in a saucepan. Cook over medium heat, stirring, for several minutes, until the coffee has dissolved completely.

3. Remove from the heat and stir in the sugar and chopped walnuts. Let cool until you can stick your finger in it, then beat in the egg with a wooden spoon until well combined. Stir in the flour just to combine.

4. Spoon the batter into the prepared loaf tin, smoothing over the top. Bake in the center of the oven for 40 minutes, or until risen and a toothpick inserted in the center comes out clean.

5. Leave to cool in the tin for 5 minutes, then turn out onto a wire rack to cool completely.

To make the coffee buttercream icing

6. Combine the butter, sugar, coffee, and 1 teaspoon of milk in a bowl and beat together until thick and creamy, adding only enough milk to give you a proper spreading consistency.

7. Spread the icing over the top of the cooled loaf and then decorate with toasted walnut halves. This cake will keep tightly covered for up to 4 days.

Battenberg Cake

This traditional teatime bake has been appearing in British cookery books for over two centuries. Another name for it is church window cake, as the finished cake is thought to resemble the appearance of the stained-glass windows of a church. It only looks complicated and is much easier to make than one would suppose. *Makes 1 (7-inch square) cake*

PREP TIME: 45 minutes, plus 45 minutes to cool BAKE TIME: 30 minutes

¾ cup (1½ sticks/ 170 grams) butter, softened

Scant 1 cup (175 grams) fine granulated sugar (caster sugar), plus more for dusting

3 large free-range eggs, lightly beaten

1¼ cups (175 grams) self-rising flour (see tip on page 22)

A few drops red food coloring

2 to 3 tablespoons vanilla buttercream icing

2 to 3 tablespoons warmed and sieved apricot jam

⅔ pound (275 grams) natural almond paste (marzipan)

1. Preheat the oven to 325°F/160°C. Generously butter a 7-inch square tin, line with parchment paper, and set aside.

2. Using an electric hand mixer or a stand mixer, beat the butter and sugar together until light and fluffy. Beat in the eggs, a little bit at a time. If the mixture curdles, add a spoonful of the flour. Stir in the flour until smooth.

3. Transfer half the batter to a separate bowl. Tint one bowl of batter pink using a few drops of red food coloring.

4. Spoon the batters into the prepared baking tin, placing the plain batter on one side and the pink batter on the other side. Smooth the top gently without mingling the batters into each other.

5. Bake on the center rack for 30 to 35 minutes. When done, the top should spring back when lightly touched near the center, and a toothpick inserted in the center should come out clean.

6. Cool in the pan for 5 minutes, then carefully tip out the dough onto a wire rack to finish cooling.

7. Once the cake is completely cool, using a serrated knife, trim all the edges away from the cake, and then cut the cake into 4 equal long sections, 2 plain and 2 pink.

8. Place one of each color cake section side by side and spread a little buttercream icing between them to help them adhere. Repeat with other 2 sections. Spread a little warm jam on top of one of the 2-section blocks and place the other 2-section block on the jam, alternating the colors for a checkerboard pattern.

9. Dust the countertop with some granulated sugar. Roll the marzipan out on the granulated sugar into a thin oblong layer, about 7 inches long and roughly wide enough to wrap all the way around the cake with about a ½-inch overlap. Brush with some of the warm apricot jam.

10. Place the checkerboard sponge on top of the marzipan, placing it into the middle, perpendicular to the short side of the marzipan rectangle. Bring the marzipan up over the cake to cover it completely and press it lightly into place, with a bit of an overlap in the center. Brush more jam on the overlap so it seals shut and holds in place.

11. Place the cake on a serving plate, seam-side down. Using the dull edge of a knife, lightly mark the top of the marzipan in the traditional crisscross pattern. Cut into slices to serve. Store any leftovers in an airtight container for up to 4 days.

Classic Lemon Drizzle Cake

I cannot think of anyone who does not immediately get excited at the sight of a lemon drizzle cake, buttery and moist with a tart lemon syrup glaze. Enjoy it cut into thick slices to serve along with hot cups of tea. *Makes 1 (8-by-4-inch) loaf*

PREP TIME: 10 minutes **BAKE TIME:** 40 minutes

For the cake
¾ cup
  (1½ sticks/170 grams)
  butter, softened
Scant 1 cup (175 grams)
  fine granulated sugar
  (caster sugar)

3 large free-range eggs,
  lightly beaten
1¼ cups (175 grams)
  self-rising flour (see tip
  on page 22), sifted
Finely grated zest and
  juice of 1 medium lemon

For the drizzle
¼ cup (50 grams) fine
  granulated sugar
  (caster sugar)
Finely grated zest and
  juice of 1 medium lemon

To make the cake

1. Preheat the oven to 350°F/180°C. Butter an 8-by-4-inch loaf tin and then line it with parchment paper, overlapping the edges for ease of removal. Set aside.

2. Using an electric hand mixer or a stand mixer, beat the butter and sugar until light and fluffy. Beat in the eggs one at a time, mixing them in well after each addition. If the mixture curdles, add a spoonful of the flour.

3. Gently fold in the flour and then stir in the lemon zest and juice to combine. Spoon the batter into the prepared pan and smooth over the top.

4. Bake on the center rack for 40 to 45 minutes, until well risen and golden brown. The top should spring back when lightly touched and a toothpick inserted in the center should come out clean.

5. While the cake is baking, whisk the sugar, lemon zest, and juice together until the sugar has dissolved. Set aside.

6. While the cake is still warm, prick it all over the top using the tines of a fork or a toothpick. Slowly drizzle the lemon syrup liberally and evenly over the top, allowing it to soak in.

7. Turn out the cake, lifting by the parchment, onto a wire rack and remove the paper carefully. Leave to cool completely before cutting into slices to serve. Store leftovers tightly covered for up to 3 days.

Madeira Cake

Contrary to the title, this delicious cake contains no madeira, nor is it related to Madeira in Portugal. It is one of the more popular British cakes, being dense and delicious and lightly flavored with lemon. I find it to be similar in texture to a North American pound cake. Traditionally it is decorated in the center with long strips of candied lemon peel. It goes down well with a hot cup of tea. *Makes 1 (8-by-4-inch) loaf cake*

PREP TIME: 15 minutes **BAKE TIME:** 1 hour

Heaping ¾ cup (115 grams) all-purpose flour

Heaping ¾ cup (115 grams) self-rising flour (see tip on page 22)

Scant 1 cup (175 grams) fine granulated sugar (caster sugar)

Finely grated zest of 1 medium lemon

¾ cup (1½ sticks/170 grams) butter, softened

3 large free-range eggs, lightly beaten

1 to 2 tablespoons whole milk

Thin slivers candied lemon peel, for garnish

Icing (confectioners') sugar, for dusting (optional)

1. Preheat the oven to 350°F/180°C. Generously butter an 8-by-4-inch loaf tin. Line with parchment paper, and set aside.

2. Sift both flours together into a bowl and set aside.

3. Measure the sugar into another bowl and rub the lemon zest into it until very fragrant. Drop in the butter and, using an electric hand mixer or stand mixer, cream together until light and fluffy. Beat in the eggs, a little bit at a time, until well incorporated. If the mixture curdles, beat in a spoonful of the flour. Fold in the flours using a metal spoon until thoroughly incorporated. Stir in just enough milk for a soft, droppable batter.

4. Spoon the batter into the prepared pan, smoothing over the top. Bake on the center rack for 20 minutes.

5. Carefully remove from the oven and lay the lemon peel on top, then return the cake to the oven to bake for 40 additional minutes, until golden brown and a toothpick inserted in the center comes out clean. Cool in the tin for 10 minutes before transferring to a wire rack to cool completely.

6. If desired, dust the cake with icing sugar before cutting into thin slices to serve. Store any leftovers in an airtight container for up to 5 days.

Traditional Swiss Roll

This is a childhood favorite: a delicious fat-free sponge, rolled up with a jam filling and cut into thick slices to serve. Of course, you can get a bit more creative and fill it with lemon curd, whipped cream, fresh fruit, and so on. It is a quick and easy cake to make. You will need a 9-by-13-inch Swiss roll tin to bake this in. *Serves 6 to 8*

PREP TIME: 10 minutes **BAKE TIME:** 10 minutes

4 large free-range eggs
½ cup (95 grams) fine
  granulated sugar (caster
  sugar), plus more
  for dusting

¾ cup (105 grams)
  self-rising flour (see tip
  on page 22)

Heaping ¼ cup straw-
  berry or raspberry jam

1. Preheat the oven to 425°F/220°C. Lightly butter a 9-by-13-inch Swiss roll tin, line the bottom with parchment paper, and set aside.

2. Combine the eggs and sugar in the bowl of a stand mixer, and using the whisk on high, whisk them together until light and frothy. Continue to mix on high until the mixture leaves a ribbon trail when you lift the whisk from the bowl. (Alternatively, you can use an electric hand mixer, although it may take you longer.)

3. Using a spatula, fold in the flour a little bit at a time, and take care not to knock the air out of the egg/sugar mixture. Don't overmix or the cake will be tough and not as light. Pour into the prepared baking tin and gently shake to level it out, making sure the batter gets into all the corners. This is import-ant because of the short bake time and high temperature.

4. Bake in the center of the oven for 10 minutes, until the cake is golden brown and the edges have begun to shrink away from the sides of the pan.

5. Meanwhile, lay out a sheet of parchment paper larger than the baking tin on the countertop and liberally dust it with sugar.

6. Invert the baked cake onto the sugar-dusted parchment paper. Remove the tin and, working quickly, carefully peel off the parchment paper. Make a shallow cut/score along one short edge of the cake, about 1 inch from the edge. Do not cut all the way through; this is only for ease of rolling. Leave to cool for a few minutes.

7. Spread a layer of jam all over the surface of the warm cake and, starting at the short edge where you made the cut, start to roll up the cake firmly.

8. Place the roll on a cake dish or platter, seam-side down. Cool completely before cutting into slices with a serrated knife to serve. Store any leftovers in an airtight container for up to 3 days.

Sticky Toffee Cake

Not to be confused with the pudding, this delightful cake embodies all of the elements of the perennial British favorite sticky toffee pudding. It has the same rich, moist date and brown sugar cake topped off with a lush brown sugar and cream frosting. *Makes 1 (7-by-11-inch) cake*

PREP TIME: 15 minutes, plus 1 hour to cool **BAKE TIME:** 45 minutes total

For the cake
8 ounces (225 grams)
   pitted Medjool dates
1¼ cups (300 mL) water
1 teaspoon baking soda
Heaping ¾ cup
   (170 grams) soft light
   brown sugar, packed
½ cup (1 stick/110 grams)
   butter, softened

1 teaspoon vanilla extract
2 large free-range eggs,
   lightly beaten
1⅓ cups (190 grams)
   self-rising flour (see tip
   on page 22)

For the icing
½ cup (100 grams)
   soft light brown
   sugar, packed
6 tablespoons (90 mL)
   heavy cream
2 tablespoons butter,
   softened
3½ tablespoons icing
   (confectioners')
   sugar, sifted

To make the cake

1. Preheat the oven to 350°F/180°C. Butter a 7-by-11-inch baking tin, line the base with parchment paper, and set aside.

2. Using a pair of kitchen scissors, snip each date into 3 or 4 pieces. Put the dates in a saucepan along with the water. Bring to a boil and boil for about 10 minutes, until most of the water has been absorbed and the dates have softened. Remove from the heat and stir in the baking soda. Set aside to cool.

3. Using a wooden spoon, cream together the brown sugar, butter, and vanilla extract until light and fluffy. Gradually beat in the eggs and then fold in the cooled date mixture. Stir in the flour to combine.

4. Spoon the batter into the prepared baking tin, smoothing the top over. Bake on the center rack for 30 to 35 minutes until risen and just set. Remove from the oven and cool in the tin for 15 minutes before tipping out onto a wire rack to cool completely.

To make the icing

5. Combine the sugar, cream, and butter in a saucepan. Heat over medium-low heat, stirring, until the sugar has dissolved. Bring to a boil, then leave to cook without stirring for exactly 4 minutes, until golden brown. Remove from the heat and allow to cool completely.

6. When cold, beat in the icing sugar until smooth. Using the back of a wet metal spoon, smooth it over top of the cold date cake. Leave to set before cutting into bars to serve. Store any leftovers in an airtight container for up to 5 days.

Traditional Christmas Cake

All over Great Britain, people go to great lengths to bake a beautiful fruitcake every year for Christmas. It is usually baked in early November, five to six weeks before Christmas, then wrapped in a brandy-soaked cloth and fed with more brandy biweekly up until the day it is savored. These are often covered with a layer of marzipan as well as a fondant icing and decorated with ribbons and small figures for the day, and served cut into thin slices late in the afternoon on Christmas Day. Many people enjoy theirs with some crumbled cheese on the side. *Makes 1 (9-inch round) cake*

PREP TIME: 15 minutes, plus overnight to soak **BAKE TIME:** 4½ hours

3 cups (450 grams) dried currants

1 generous cup (175 grams) raisins

1 generous cup (175 grams) sultanas

¼ cup (50 grams) glacé cherries, rinsed, dried, and halved

¼ cup (50 grams) finely chopped candied citrus peel (see tip)

⅓ cup (80 mL) good brandy, plus more for soaking the cake

1⅔ cups (225 grams) all-purpose flour

½ teaspoon mixed spice (see page 8)

¼ teaspoon freshly grated nutmeg

Pinch salt

1 cup (2 sticks/225 grams) butter

1 cup plus 2 tablespoons (225 grams) soft light brown sugar, packed

4 large free-range eggs, lightly beaten

2 tablespoons dark molasses

¼ cup (50 grams) coarsely chopped blanched almonds

Finely grated zest of 1 medium lemon

Finely grated zest of 1 medium orange

1. The evening before you are going to bake the cake, combine the currants, raisins, and sultanas in a large glass bowl, along with the cherries and candied citrus peel. Mix well and then stir in the brandy. Cover the bowl with a plate and leave to sit overnight, giving it an occasional stir.

2. In the morning, preheat the oven to 275°F/140°C. Generously butter a deep 9-inch round baking tin and then line it with 2 layers of parchment paper, buttering each layer. Set aside.

3. Sift the flour into a bowl along with the mixed spice, nutmeg, and salt. Set aside.

4. In a separate bowl, cream the butter and brown sugar together until light and fluffy, using an electric hand mixer. Beat in the eggs, a little bit at a time. If the mixture curdles, add a spoonful of the flour mixture. Fold in the flour mixture to combine well.

5. Fold in the dark molasses along with the steeped fruits and any brandy left in the bowl, the chopped almonds, and the grated citrus zests. Mix well and then spread the mixture into the prepared pan, pressing it down lightly. Place the prepared baking tin on a baking sheet.

6. Take a double thickness of newspaper and tie it around the outside of the cake tin, making sure it extends about an inch above the tin. Top with a large square of parchment paper with a 1-inch hole cut out of the center.

7. Place the tray with the cake tin on the lowest rack of the oven. Bake for 4½ to 4¾ hours, until the cake springs back when lightly touched and a toothpick inserted in the center comes out clean.

8. Place the cake, in the tin, on a wire rack to cool for 30 minutes, then remove the newspaper and discard. Carefully tip the cake out onto the wire rack and remove the baking parchment. Let cool completely.

9. Soak a double thickness of cheesecloth in some brandy and wrap the cake in this. Place into a tin, tightly cover, and leave in a dark spot until ready to decorate. Spoon a few tablespoons of brandy over the top of it twice a week until then.

Ingredient Tip: I like to order my candied citrus peels whole and then chop them myself. You can purchase them online. See page 76 for a recipe to make your own.

Technique Tip: Don't stint on the recommended paper linings and wrappings for the cake. Because of the long, slow cooking, these are necessary to help keep the cake moist.

DIY Candied Citrus Peels

If you are really keen on candied citrus peels, you can make your own. You will need the peels of citrus fruits, such as grapefruit, oranges, lemons, etc. Remove the peels and a fair amount (not too thick) of the pith (the bitter white part). Blanch the peels several times in boiling water. To do this, cut the peels into strips and put them in a saucepan. Cover with cold water, bring to a boil for 5 minutes, and drain. Repeat this process three times. If your peels still taste quite bitter, repeat again. Grapefruit peels sometimes need to be blanched a few more times.

Once they are blanched, make a simple syrup by using equal parts water and granulated sugar, enough to completely submerge your peels. Bring the water and sugar to a boil, allow the sugar to dissolve completely, and then add the peels. Reduce to a simmer and simmer the peels until soft and slightly translucent, 45 minutes to 1 hour.

Set up a drying rack over some parchment paper. Carefully remove the peels from the syrup and lay them out in a single layer on the drying rack. Leave them to dry overnight. (Keep any syrup left in the pan. It makes a great sweetener for teas or other beverages.) Optionally, once the peel has dried, you can roll it in granulated sugar to coat, but it is lovely just as it is.

Store the candied peel in an airtight container in a cool, dark place for several months.

Bara Brith

Bara brith is a Welsh quick bread/cake. It contains no fat at all, yet it's incredibly moist and delicious. Loaded with fruit, this treat is fabulous cut into thin slices and served with soft butter for spreading. You will need to plan ahead, as the fruit needs to soak overnight in cold tea. *Makes 1 (8-by-4-inch) loaf*

PREP TIME: 15 minutes, plus overnight to soak **BAKE TIME:** 2 hours

2½ cups (350 grams) mixed dried fruits (raisins, sultanas, currants)

1¼ cups (300 mL) strongly brewed tea, cold

1¾ cups (250 grams) all-purpose flour

2 teaspoons baking powder

2 teaspoons mixed spice (see page 8)

Pinch salt

⅔ cup (130 grams) fine granulated sugar (caster sugar)

1 large free-range egg, lightly beaten

1. Put the dried fruit in a bowl. Pour the cold tea over top and stir to combine. Cover the bowl with a plate and leave to sit overnight. Do not drain.

2. The next morning, preheat the oven to 350°F/180°C. Butter an 8-by-4-inch loaf tin and line the bottom and up both long sides with parchment paper, leaving an overhang for ease of lifting out. Set aside.

3. Sift the flour, baking powder, mixed spice, and salt together into a bowl. Stir in the sugar to combine.

4. Add the soaked fruit, along with any juices in the bowl, and the beaten egg. Mix well.

5. Spoon the batter into the prepared loaf tin, smoothing the top level. Bake in the center of the oven for 2 hours, until well risen and golden brown. A toothpick inserted in the center should come out clean. Cool in the tin for 10 minutes before lifting the loaf out to a wire rack to cool completely. Store in an airtight container for up to 2 weeks.

Scottish Dundee Cake

Dundee cake is a traditional Scottish fruitcake. Unlike the Traditional Christmas Cake (page 74), this has a light batter and no candied cherries in it, containing only raisins and currants. It is not quite as labor-intensive as the traditional fruitcake, but it's every bit as delicious. The top is decorated with whole blanched almonds. *Makes 1 (7-inch round) cake*

PREP TIME: 15 minutes **BAKE TIME:** 2 hours 15 minutes

1¼ cups (175 grams) self-rising flour (see tip on page 22), sifted

½ teaspoon mixed spice (see page 8)

Pinch salt

Scant 1 cup (175 grams) fine granulated sugar (caster sugar)

Finely grated zest of 1 large orange

¾ cup plus 1 tablespoon (175 grams) butter

3 large free-range eggs, lightly beaten

1 cup (150 grams) dried currants

1 cup (150 grams) raisins

6 tablespoons (80 grams) chopped mixed candied citrus peel

1 tablespoon Scottish whisky

16 to 20 whole blanched almonds

1. Preheat the oven to 325°F/160°C. Butter a deep 7-inch round cake tin, line with parchment paper, and set aside.

2. Sift together the flour, mixed spice, and salt. Set aside.

3. Rub the sugar and orange zest together until fragrant. Add the butter and beat together until light and fluffy. Beat in the eggs, a little bit at a time, until thoroughly combined. If the mixture curdles, stir in a teaspoon of the flour mixture. Stir in the flour mixture thoroughly. Stir in the currants, raisins, and candied peel along with the whisky, combining well.

4. Spoon into the prepared baking tin, smoothing over the top. Bake for 1½ hours. Remove from the oven and place the blanched almonds decoratively on top in two concentric circles. Return the cake to the oven and bake for an additional 45 minutes. The cake is done when golden brown and a toothpick inserted in the center comes out clean. Transfer to a wire rack and allow to cool completely before removing from the cake tin. Store in an airtight container for up to a month.

CHAPTER 5

Sweet and Savory Pies and Tarts

Cornish Pasties, 84

Sausage Rolls

These classic puff pastry rolls filled with a savory sausage filling are popular all over the UK. They are great for parties, picnics, lunches, and game nights. Cut into smaller pieces, they also make great appetizers. *Makes 12*

PREP TIME: 10 minutes **BAKE TIME:** 15 minutes

1¼ pounds (500 grams) good-quality sausage meat

1 large onion, minced

¾ cup (90 grams) fine dry bread crumbs

1 large free-range egg, beaten and divided

Salt

Freshly ground black pepper

1 sheet ready-made all-butter puff pastry, thawed if frozen

All-purpose flour, for dusting

1. Preheat the oven to 425°F/220°C. Line a large baking sheet with parchment paper and set aside.

2. Crumble the sausage meat into a bowl. Add the minced onion, bread crumbs, and half of the beaten egg, along with some salt and pepper. Mix everything together well, using your hands to combine. Divide the mixture into 3 equal portions.

3. Unroll the puff pastry and lay it out on a lightly floured countertop. Using a lightly floured rolling pin, roll the pastry out to a 12-by-16-inch rectangle. Cut the rectangle crosswise into 3 long strips.

4. Shape each third of the sausage meat mixture into a log the length of each strip of pastry, by rolling it between the palms of your hands. Place one meat log down the center of each pastry strip.

5. Brush one long edge of each strip with some of the remaining beaten egg. Roll the pastry up over the meat to enclose, overlapping the edges with the egg-brushed edge facing down on the bottom edge. Gently press closed.

6. Carefully flip the logs over and flatten them slightly with the palm of your hand. Cut each crosswise into 4 even pieces and place them onto the prepared baking sheet, leaving some space in between each. Brush the top of each sausage roll with the remainder of the beaten egg and snip the dough on top a couple of times with kitchen scissors to vent. Alternatively, you can prick each with a fork a few times.

7. Bake for 15 to 20 minutes, until golden brown and cooked through.

Variation Tip: For sausage and cheese rolls, add 1 cup (120 grams) grated cheese to the sausage mix. Stilton is nice, as is a good cheddar. For a fruited sausage roll, you can add half of a medium apple (peeled and grated) or ½ cup (75 grams) chopped dried cranberries or apricots to the sausage mix.

Cornish Pasties

Pasties are a type of meat and potato pie that have long been associated with the Cornwall area of the UK and hold a protected geographical status (PGI). Shaped like a half-moon, this sturdy pastry is crimped on the side rather than the top and contains a delicious meat, potato, rutabaga, and onion filling. These are meant to be eaten by hand and are wonderful for picnics or bagged lunches! Do plan ahead, as the pastry needs to chill for at least 3 hours prior to baking. *Makes 6*

PREP TIME: 25 minutes, plus 3 hours to chill **BAKE TIME:** 50 minutes

3⅔ cups (500 grams) strong bread flour (high-gluten flour), plus more for dusting

1 teaspoon salt, plus more to taste

½ cup (110 grams) lard or white vegetable shortening, cut into bits

½ cup (1 stick/110 grams) butter, cut into bits

Scant ¾ cup (175 mL) cold water

1 pound (450 grams) flank steak, cut into small dice

1 pound (450 grams) potatoes, peeled and cut into small dice

8 ounces (225 grams) rutabaga, peeled and cut into small dice

1 large onion, thinly sliced

Freshly ground black pepper

1 medium free-range egg, beaten with 1 tablespoon water

1. Sift the flour and salt into a bowl. Drop the lard and butter into the flour. Rub the fat into the flour using your fingertips until the mixture resembles fine bread crumbs. Using a fork, stir in the cold water until the mixture comes together.

2. Tip the dough out onto a lightly floured countertop and knead the pastry until quite elastic. (This is in opposition to how you normally handle pastry, but it is necessary for a strong enough pastry to hold the filling and keep its shape.) Wrap the pastry in plastic wrap and chill in the refrigerator for 3 hours.

3. Preheat the oven to 325°F/160°C. Line a rimmed baking sheet with parchment paper.

4. Remove the pastry from the refrigerator and divide it into 6 equal pieces. Roll each piece of pastry into a round roughly 8 inches in diameter.

5. Layer the meat and vegetables on half of each pastry, seasoning each layer with salt and pepper as you go. Bring the other half of the pastry over the top to cover the filling, crimping the edges shut (see tip). Brush the top of each pasty with some of the egg wash and make a few slashes in the top with a sharp knife to vent.

6. Place the filled pastries on a the prepared baking sheet. Bake for 50 to 55 minutes, until the pasties are golden brown and the filling is cooked through.

Technique Tip: To crimp the edges, lightly brush the edge of the pastry with some water and squeeze tightly together. Using your index finger and thumb, twist the edges of the pastry over to shape, folding it over on itself and continuing down the edge until it is all crimped. Tuck the corners underneath to hold them in place.

Steak and Mushroom Pie

You will find a good steak and mushroom pie offered at just about every pub across the length and breadth of the UK. Imagine tender meat and mushrooms in a rich gravy with a puff pastry topping. What's not to love? You can make this a real feast with a mound of fluffy mashed potatoes and a cooked vegetable on the side. *Serves 6*

PREP TIME: 15 minutes   **COOK/BAKE TIME:** 2 hours 45 minutes

3 pounds (1360 grams) stewing beef, cut into 1-inch cubes

3 tablespoons all-purpose flour

Salt

Freshly ground black pepper

2 tablespoons canola oil

1 large onion, finely diced

3 carrots, peeled and finely diced

2 celery stalks, finely diced

12 ounces (340 grams) button mushrooms (such as cremini or chestnut mushrooms), halved

4 garlic cloves, minced

2 cups (480 mL) good beef stock

4 fresh thyme sprigs

1 fresh rosemary sprig

2 dried bay leaves

1 teaspoon sweet paprika

1 sheet ready-made all-butter puff pastry, thawed if frozen

1 medium free-range egg, beaten with 1 teaspoon water

1. Toss the beef cubes together with the flour and salt and black pepper to taste.

2. Heat the oil in a large pan over medium-high heat. Add the beef in small batches and brown it on all sides. As the beef browns, transfer it to a bowl and set aside.

3. Add the onion, carrots, and celery to the pan drippings. Cook over medium heat until soft and very fragrant. Add the mushrooms and the garlic to the pan and cook, stirring occasionally, for about 5 minutes, until they begin to soften.

4. Add the stock, thyme, rosemary, bay leaves, and paprika. Return the beef to the pot, along with any juices that have accumulated, and stir to make sure everything is well combined. Cover tightly and simmer gently for 1½ to 2 hours, stirring every now and then, until the meat is beautifully tender. If you think the liquid is reducing too much, add more stock.

5. Uncover, reduce the heat, and simmer the mixture for an additional 20 minutes at a slow bubble to reduce and thicken the mixture slightly. Taste and adjust the seasoning as required. Remove and discard the bay leaves and herb stems.

6. Preheat the oven to 350°F/180°C.

7. Pour the meat filling into a large shallow casserole dish, spreading it out evenly.

8. Unroll the pastry and cover the filling with the pastry, crimping the edges decoratively all the way around. Cut a few slits in the top to vent and brush all over with the egg-water glaze.

9. Bake for 25 to 30 minutes, until the pastry is nicely puffed, cooked through, and golden brown. Remove the pie from the oven and allow to rest for about 10 minutes before serving. To serve, cut the pastry into squares. Spoon a portion of the filling onto heated plates and top each serving with a square of pastry.

Technique Tip: Cooking your meat in small batches will result in a nice golden-brown sear, which will add plenty of flavor to your finished dish.

Eccles Cakes

I first tasted these lovely pastries back in the 1980s. It was love at first bite. The simple recipe was given to me by a girl from the Northwest of England. Who can resist delicious little dried fruit–filled delicacies encased in flaky pastry? Not I! The original recipe comes from the town of Eccles, which is located in Lancashire. *Makes 2 dozen*

PREP TIME: 15 minutes **BAKE TIME:** 10 minutes

3 tablespoons butter, melted

⅓ cup (45 grams) dried currants

⅓ cup (45 grams) raisins

6 tablespoons (75 grams) soft light or dark brown sugar, packed

5 tablespoons (65 grams) chopped mixed candied peel (see tip)

Finely grated zest of 1 medium orange

½ teaspoon ground cinnamon

¼ teaspoon freshly grated nutmeg

All-purpose flour, for dusting

2 batches Flaky Pastry (page 90)

1 medium free-range egg, beaten with 1 teaspoon water

2 tablespoons whole milk, for brushing

3 tablespoons demerara sugar, for sprinkling

1. Preheat the oven to 400°F/200°C. Line a rimmed baking sheet with parchment paper and set aside.

2. Mix the melted butter, currants, raisins, brown sugar, candied peel, zest, cinnamon, and nutmeg in a bowl, combining them well. Set aside.

3. Using a lightly floured rolling pin, roll out the pastry on a lightly floured surface to ⅛ inch thickness. Cut out rounds using a 3¼-inch cookie cutter.

4. Place 1 heaping teaspoon of the filling in the center of each round. Brush the edges of each round with some egg wash, then bring them together in the center, wrapping up the filling and pressing the edges firmly together. Turn the discs over

and flatten them slightly between the palms of your hands until you have a little pastry roughly 2 inches in diameter. Place them 2 inches apart on the prepared baking sheet. Gather up and re-roll scraps of pastry as needed.

5. Brush the tops of each pastry with milk and sprinkle with a bit of demerara sugar. Using a sharp knife, cut 2 small slits in the top of each pastry.

6. Bake for 10 to 15 minutes, until golden brown. Scoop off onto a wire rack to cool completely before serving. Store any leftovers in an airtight container for up to 3 days.

Ingredient Tip: You can purchase candied citrus peels whole and then chop them yourself. See page 76 for a recipe to make your own.

Flaky Pastry

This is a quick and easy alternative to puff pastry and makes a great casing for pies, turnovers, and tarts. You can make it ahead and freeze for convenience. *Makes 8 ounces (225 grams)*

PREP TIME: 15 minutes, plus 30 minutes to chill

1⅔ cups (225 grams) all-purpose flour, plus more for dusting

⅛ teaspoon fine sea salt

2 tablespoons fine granulated sugar (caster sugar) (if using for a sweet bake)

¾ cup (1½ sticks/ 170 grams) butter, softened

¼ to ½ cup (60 to 120 mL) cold water

1. Sift the flour and salt into a bowl. Stir in the sugar, if using.

2. Divide the butter into 4 equal portions. Add one portion of butter to the flour mixture and incorporate it using a butter knife, along with just enough cold water for a soft dough that is not sticky.

3. Tip the dough out onto a lightly floured surface. Using a floured rolling pin, roll the dough into a rectangle roughly ¼ inch thick.

4. Using a pastry brush, brush off any excess flour from the surface of the dough. Cut another portion of the butter into bits and evenly space over two-thirds of the surface of the pastry. Fold the pastry in thirds, bringing the end third without the butter to the center first and covering with the opposite end.

5. Press the edges together with your fingers and then give the pastry a half turn. Roll out again to a rectangle ¼ inch thick.

6. Repeat steps 4 and 5 two more times until you have used up all the butter. Wrap in plastic wrap and chill in the refrigerator for 30 minutes, then proceed as directed in the recipe you are using it in. Alternatively, you can wrap the pastry tightly and freeze for up to 3 months. Thaw in the refrigerator overnight before using.

Bakewell Tart

This delicious tart hails from a town in the Derbyshire region of the UK. It consists of a lovely puff pastry base filled with raspberry jam and a delicious almond frangipane, which is topped and baked with flaked almonds.

Makes 1 (8-inch) tart

PREP TIME: 15 minutes **BAKE TIME:** 30 minutes

All-purpose flour, for dusting

1 sheet ready-made all-butter puff pastry, thawed if frozen

2 tablespoons raspberry jam

2 large free-range eggs plus 2 additional egg yolks

7 tablespoons (95 grams) butter, melted

½ cup (95 grams) fine granulated sugar (caster sugar)

½ cup (50 grams) ground almonds

2 tablespoons flaked almonds, for sprinkling

1 tablespoon icing (confectioners') sugar, for dusting

1. Preheat the oven to 400°F/200°C. Butter an 8-inch tart tin or flan ring.

2. Roll the pastry out on a lightly floured surface, using a lightly floured rolling pin, to a round large enough to line the tart tin (roughly 11 inches in diameter). Line the tart tin with the pastry, taking care not to stretch it (see tip). Trim the pastry to fit and flute the edges. Spread the raspberry jam over the pastry in an even layer.

3. Using a wooden spoon, beat together the whole eggs, egg yolks, melted butter, sugar, and ground almonds. Spoon the egg mixture into the tart tin and spread to cover the jam. Sprinkle the flaked almonds evenly over top.

4. Bake for 30 minutes, until the filling is firm to the touch. It should spring back when lightly touched. Cool completely, then dust with a bit of icing sugar and cut into wedges to serve.

Treacle Tart

Treacle is another name for golden syrup, which is a much-beloved sweetener used in the UK. It has a unique flavor with almost a hint of lemon. This tart used to be made with dark treacle, which is like a very strong molasses, but you never see that being done anymore. *Serves 8*

PREP TIME: 15 minutes **BAKE TIME:** 35 minutes

12 ounces (350 grams) Sweet Short Crust Pastry (page 93)
2 cups (480 mL) golden syrup
Finely grated zest and juice of 1 medium lemon

3¾ cups (225 grams) fresh soft white bread crumbs
1 pear or apple, peeled, cored, and grated
1 teaspoon mixed spice (see page 8)

1 large egg yolk beaten with ½ teaspoon cold water
Heavy cream or vanilla ice cream, for serving

1. Preheat the oven to 350°F/180°C.

2. Using a lightly floured rolling pin, roll three-quarters of the pastry out on a lightly floured surface to a round large enough to line a 10-inch flan dish. Carefully transfer the pastry to the flan dish and gently knock the pastry into place using your knuckles.

3. Combine the golden syrup, lemon zest, and juice in a saucepan. Warm gently, then stir in the bread crumbs, grated pear, and mixed spice. Pour over the prepared pastry.

4. Roll the remaining quarter of the pastry out to ¼ inch thickness and cut into strips about ⅓ inch wide. Lay the strips in a lattice pattern on top of the tart, crimping the edges of the tart all the way around with the tines of a fork, and pressing the lattice strips into place. Brush the lattice and edges of the tart with the egg wash.

5. Bake for 35 minutes, until the pastry is crisp and golden brown and the filling has set. Serve warm, cut into wedges and topped with a drizzle of heavy cream or a scoop of vanilla ice cream.

Sweet Short Crust Pastry

This basic pastry works well for all manner of sweet pies. *Makes 1 pound*

PREP TIME: 10 minutes, plus 30 minutes to chill

1⅔ cups (225 grams) all-purpose flour
Pinch salt
⅔ cup (150 grams) butter, cut into bits

6 tablespoons fine granulated sugar (caster sugar) or icing (confectioners') sugar

1 large free-range egg plus 1 additional egg yolk

1. Sift the flour and salt into a bowl. Drop in the butter and rub it in using your fingertips to make a mixture similar to medium-fine dry bread crumbs. Stir in the sugar.

2. Beat the egg and egg yolk together. Add to the flour mixture and work everything together until it becomes a smooth dough, kneading briefly. Shape into a disk and wrap tightly in plastic wrap. Chill for 30 to 60 minutes prior to using.

Technique Tip: The number one cause of tough pastry is overhandling. A gentle touch is key when it comes to making a flaky pastry.

Banoffee Pie

This scrumptious pie is a real favorite in the UK, quite similar to the refrigerator pies of North America. A digestive biscuit crust is topped with sliced banana, a rich caramel filling, and a layer of sweet whipped cream. Making the caramel filling does take a bit of time, but it is well worth it. The most difficult part is waiting for it to chill. You will need two baking dishes to make the bain-marie (water bath) for the caramel filling; one must fit inside the other. *Makes 8 servings*

PREP TIME: 15 minutes, plus 4 hours to cool and chill **BAKE TIME:** 1½ hours

1½ cups (135 grams) Digestive Biscuit crumbs (page 20) or graham cracker crumbs

10 tablespoons (1¼ sticks/280 grams) butter, softened

2 (14-ounce/400 grams) cans sweetened condensed milk (not evaporated milk)

3 large ripe bananas

1½ cups (360 mL) heavy cream

⅓ cup (43 grams) icing (confectioners') sugar, sifted

1 teaspoon vanilla extract

2 tablespoons grated semisweet chocolate, for decorating

1. Preheat the oven to 350°F/180°C.

2. Mix the crumbs and butter together for the crust. Press the mixture evenly into a 9-inch pie plate. Bake for 5 to 8 minutes, until light golden brown. Remove from the oven and set aside to cool.

3. Reduce the oven temperature to 300°F/150°C.

4. Pour the condensed milk into a 9-by-13-by-2-inch glass baking dish. Cover tightly with aluminum foil. Place the covered dish in a larger baking dish or roasting pan. Add boiling water to the larger dish to come roughly halfway up the sides of the smaller dish. Carefully place both in the oven and bake for 1½ hours.

5. Remove the dishes from the oven and carefully remove the dish containing the caramel from the dish containing the hot water. Uncover and set aside to cool completely.

6. Spread half of the cooled caramel filling into the cooled crumb crust. Slice the bananas over the top and cover with the remainder of the caramel filling, spreading it evenly.

7. Whip the cream together with the icing sugar and vanilla until it forms soft peaks. Spread over the top of the filling and bananas. Sprinkle with the grated chocolate. Chill for several hours.

Creamy Caramel Custard Tart

This old English recipe (sometimes called a gypsy tart) is said to have originated on the Isle of Sheppey in the county of Kent. It is rich and sweet. Other than the pastry, it contains only two ingredients and was often considered to be the highlight of school dinners back in the day! It does take quite a while to whip the brown sugar and the milk together, so be forewarned. This is when a stand mixer comes in very handy! *Makes 1 (9-inch) tart*

PREP TIME: 35 minutes **BAKE TIME:** 40 minutes

All-purpose flour,
  for dusting
175 grams (about
  ½ recipe) Sweet Short
  Crust Pastry (page 93)
1⅔ cups (400 mL)
  evaporated milk

(not sweetened
  condensed milk)
1½ cups (300 grams)
  soft light brown sugar,
  packed, or demer-
  ara sugar

1⅓ cups (320 mL)
  heavy cream
Finely grated zest
  of 1 lemon

1. Butter a deep 9-inch tart tin with a removable bottom and set aside.

2. Using a lightly floured rolling pin, roll out the pastry on a lightly floured surface to ¼ inch thickness. Line the prepared tart tin with the pastry, gently knocking in the edges with your knuckles. Leave an overhang (see tip). Place in the refrigerator to chill for 30 minutes.

3. Preheat the oven to 350°F/180°C. Remove the pastry from the refrigerator. Prick the pastry in a few places with a fork. Line the top of the pastry with parchment paper and then fill with pie weights or dried beans.

4. Bake for 20 minutes. Remove the parchment and pie weights, return the crust to the oven, and bake for an additional 5 to 10 minutes, until the base is crisp and the pastry is light golden brown. Remove from the oven and trim off any excess pastry from the edge. Set aside while you make the filling. Leave the oven on.

5. To make the filling, combine the evaporated milk and brown sugar in the bowl of a stand mixer. Whisk on high until the mixture becomes light and fluffy, about 20 minutes. (Alternatively you can use an electric hand mixer.) Pour the mixture into the baked crust.

6. Bake the filled pie for 15 minutes, until risen and almost set. The surface of the tart will feel somewhat tacky, but the center should still have a bit of a jiggle. Place the tart tin on a wire rack and allow the pie to cool completely before serving.

7. When the tart is ready to serve, whip the cream with the lemon zest until it forms soft dollops. Cut the tart into wedges to serve and pass the whipped cream at the table.

Technique Tip: Do not stretch the pastry when you are moving it into your tart tin. This will help prevent it from shrinking when baked. I find it best to leave the pastry overhanging the sides of the tart tin and then trimming it off once baked.

Savory Short Crust Pastry

This basic pastry is ideal for savory pies. *Makes 14 ounces*

PREP TIME: 10 minutes, plus 30 minutes to chill

1⅔ cups (225 grams) all-purpose flour

Pinch salt

⅔ cup (150 grams) butter, cut into bits

1 large free-range egg

Scant 2 tablespoons (25 mL) water

1. Sift the flour and salt into a bowl. Drop in the butter and rub it in using your fingertips to make a mixture similar to medium-fine dry bread crumbs.

2. Whisk the egg and water together. Add to the flour mixture and work everything together until it becomes a smooth dough, kneading briefly. Shape into a disk and wrap tightly in plastic wrap. Chill for 30 to 60 minutes prior to using.

Technique Tip: The number one cause of tough pastry is overhandling. A gentle touch is key when it comes to making a flaky pastry.

Homemade Mincemeat

This is the tastiest mincemeat tart/pie filling. It is nice and fruity and beautifully spiced. Once you realize how very easy it is to make your own, you will never buy a jar of it again! *Makes 1 pound (enough for about 3 dozen mince pies)*

PREP TIME: 15 minutes, plus 12 hours to rest

1 cup (150 grams) dried currants

¾ cup packed (125 grams) raisins

⅓ cup (25 grams) blanched almonds, finely chopped

1 sweet apple, peeled, cored, and grated using the large holes of a box grater

½ cup (50 grams) shredded beef or vegetable suet (see tip)

1 knob preserved stem ginger, finely chopped (see tip)

2 tablespoons calvados (French apple brandy)

1 tablespoon dark brown sugar, packed

¼ teaspoon ground cinnamon

¼ teaspoon ground nutmeg

⅛ teaspoon ground cloves

Finely grated zest and juice of 1 medium lemon

1. Combine the currants, raisins, almonds, apple, suet, ginger, calvados, sugar, cinnamon, nutmeg, cloves, zest, and juice in a large bowl. You can use your hands to make sure everything is evenly mixed.

2. Cover the bowl with a clean towel and set aside on the counter for at least 12 hours in order to meld the flavors together. Transfer to a container with a tight-fitting lid and store in the refrigerator until ready to use.

3. Bring to room temperature prior to use.

Ingredient Tip: Suet can be purchased from any good butcher and in some grocery shops. It can also be purchased online. Alternatively, you can use an equal quantity of grated frozen vegetable shortening. Preserved stem ginger can be purchased online; try Opies Chinese Stem Ginger.

Mince Pies

These mini pies are very much a British Christmas tradition. Small, crisp, and buttery pastry cases filled with a delicious filling of spiced fruits and nuts, dusted or not with sifted icing sugar, always go down as a real treat during the holidays. You can use a ready-made mincemeat filling if you wish, but the pies are exponentially better if you make your own filling from scratch. It just wouldn't be Christmas without a few dozen or more of these to munch on!
Makes 24

PREP TIME: 25 minutes, plus 30 minutes to chill **BAKE TIME:** 25 minutes

2½ cups (350 grams) all-purpose flour, plus more for dusting

Pinch salt

⅓ cup (75 grams) cold lard, cut into bits

⅓ cup (75 grams) cold butter, cut into bits

Ice water, as needed

1¼ pounds (560 grams) mincemeat, home-made (page 99) or store-bought

Milk, for brushing

Icing (confectioners') sugar, for dusting

1. Sift the flour and salt into a large bowl. Drop in the lard and butter and rub them into the flour, using a snapping motion with your fingertips, until the mixture resembles fine dry bread crumbs. Work quickly so the fat doesn't melt into the flour.

2. Using a fork, add ice water, 1 tablespoon at a time, until the mixture forms a dough that leaves the sides of the bowl. Shape into a disk and wrap tightly in plastic wrap. Place into the refrigerator to chill for 30 minutes.

3. Preheat the oven to 400°F/200°C. Lightly butter 2 muffin tins.

4. Divide the pastry in half. Using a lightly floured rolling pin, roll half of the pastry out on a lightly floured surface to ¼ inch thickness. Cut into 24 rounds using a 3-inch fluted pastry cutter. Fit a round into each hole of the muffin tins. (They don't need to come all the way up the sides.) Fill each with 1 heaping tablespoon of mincemeat.

5. Roll the remaining pastry out in the same manner as you did the first half. Cut out 24 rounds using a 2½-inch fluted cutter. Brush the edges of each round with a bit of water and place them on top of the mincemeat-filled pastry cases, lightly pressing around the edges to seal.

6. Brush the tops with a tiny bit of milk and prick with a fork. Bake on the top rack for 25 to 30 minutes, until crisp and golden brown.

7. Remove from the oven and leave in the tins for 5 minutes, then carefully transfer to a wire rack to finish cooling completely. Dust the tops with icing sugar and store in a tightly covered container for at least a week, if not longer.

Traditional Custard Tart

This delicate, rich tart generously dusted with nutmeg is best served at room temperature, where it has a soft and creamy texture. If chilled, it loses some of its magic and flavor. It is a wonderful treat. *Makes 1 (8-inch) tart*

PREP TIME: 15 minutes **BAKE TIME:** 45 minutes

1 Sweet Short Crust Pastry (page 93)

2 cups (500 mL) whipping cream

8 large free-range egg yolks

6½ tablespoons (78 grams) fine granulated sugar (caster sugar)

Freshly grated nutmeg, for dusting

1. Preheat the oven to 350°F/180°C. Butter an 8-inch tart tin or flan pan with a removable bottom.

2. Using a lightly floured rolling pin, roll the pastry out on a lightly floured surface to ¼ inch thickness. Carefully transfer the pastry to the prepared tart tin and gently knock the pastry in using your knuckles. Leave any excess pastry hanging over the edge of the tin.

3. Line the top of the pastry with parchment paper and fill with pie weights or dried beans. Place on a baking sheet and bake for 15 minutes. Remove from the oven and reduce the oven temperature to 250°F/120°C. Remove the parchment and beans. Trim off any excess pastry and discard.

4. To make the filling, put the cream in a saucepan and bring just to a boil.

5. Whisk the egg yolks and sugar together in a bowl. Slowly pour the hot cream over the egg mixture, whisking constantly. Pass through a sieve into a large measuring cup to remove any solids, then pour the mixture into the partially baked crust. Generously grate fresh nutmeg over the top of the tart.

6. Bake for 30 to 35 minutes, just until the custard has set. It should still have a gentle wobble in the center. Cool to room temperature before serving.

Yeasted Breads

Chelsea Buns, 108

English Muffins

These round, flattish yeasted breads are baked on a griddle pan or in a skillet. Once baked, they are meant to be split open with a fork and toasted. This method of tearing them open creates lots of nooks and crannies that, once toasted, crisp up nicely, perfect for your butter to melt into. *Makes 8 to 10*

PREP TIME: 20 minutes, plus 1 hour to rise **BAKE TIME:** 15 minutes

Scant 5 cups (675 grams) strong white bread flour, plus more for dusting

2 teaspoons fine granulated sugar (caster sugar)

2¼ teaspoons fast-acting yeast

1½ teaspoons fine sea salt

Scant 2 cups (450 mL) lukewarm whole milk

1 teaspoon fine cornmeal, for dusting

Canola oil, for greasing

1. Lightly dust a large baking sheet with flour and set aside.

2. Combine the flour, sugar, yeast, and salt in the bowl of a stand mixer. Whisk together to combine by hand. Begin to pour in the milk, slowly, in a steady stream, with the mixer on low to medium. Stop the mixer and switch to a dough hook. (See tip for electric hand mixer instructions.)

3. Knead the dough using the dough hook for about 10 minutes, until the dough is smooth and elastic.

4. Turn the dough out onto a lightly floured surface and, using a lightly floured rolling pin, roll the dough out to ½ inch thickness.

5. Cut into rounds using a 3-inch cookie cutter, taking care not to twist the dough. Place the rounds on the floured baking sheet, leaving space between them to rise. Dust the tops with the cornmeal. (You can re-roll the scraps to cut more, but they won't be as perfect to look at as your first cuts, so do try to get as many as you can from the first lot.)

6. Cover loosely with lightly oiled plastic wrap and set aside in a warm place to rise until they have doubled in size, about 1 hour.

7. Lightly grease a griddle pan or a heavy-bottomed skillet with oil. Heat over medium heat until you can feel the warmth from the pan when you hold your hand about an inch over the top.

8. Place the rounds in the pan two or three at a time, then immediately turn the heat down to low. Cook on each side until golden brown and well risen, about 7 minutes per side. Scoop the muffins onto a wire rack to cool before splitting and toasting.

9. These will keep tightly wrapped or in an airtight container for up to 4 days. You can also freeze them, tightly wrapped, for up to 2 months.

Technique Tip: You can make these with an electric hand mixer if you wish. Just mix up to the kneading part and then finish them by tipping the dough out onto a lightly floured surface and kneading it by hand until the dough is smooth and elastic. Proceed as directed.

Chelsea Buns

These dense, fruited buns are as popular in the UK as cinnamon rolls are in North America. The buns were originally made and sold in the eighteenth century at the Chelsea Bun House in the Pimlico area of London. They are delicious served warm and buttered along with a nice hot cup of tea or coffee. *Makes 9*

PREP TIME: 30 minutes, plus 2 hours to rise **BAKE TIME:** 30 minutes

1⅔ cups (225 grams) strong bread flour, divided, plus more for dusting

2¼ teaspoons regular dried yeast

1 teaspoon fine granulated sugar (caster sugar)

½ cup (120 mL) warm milk

Pinch salt

1 heaping tablespoon lard, softened

1 medium free-range egg, lightly beaten

¼ cup (50 grams) butter, melted, plus more butter for greasing and serving (optional)

¼ cup (50 grams) soft light brown sugar, packed

⅓ cup (50 grams) raisins

⅓ cup (50 grams) dried currants

⅓ cup (50 grams) sultanas

¼ cup (25 grams) mixed candied peel

¼ cup (60 mL) honey

1. Combine ⅓ cup (50 grams) of flour, the yeast, sugar, and milk in a bowl. Whisk together until smooth, then cover lightly with a tea towel and set aside in a warm place for 20 minutes. It will become quite frothy.

2. Meanwhile, combine the remaining 1⅓ cups (175 grams) of flour and the salt in a separate bowl, and drop in the lard. Using your fingertips, rub the lard into the flour until well combined.

3. Stir the yeast mixture into the flour mixture along with the beaten egg to make a soft dough. Tip out the dough onto a lightly floured surface and knead for about 5 minutes, until you have a nice smooth dough. Shape into a ball.

4. Lightly oil a clean bowl and add the ball of dough, turning the dough to oil the top. Cover with a piece of plastic wrap and set aside in a warm place to rise until doubled in size, about 1½ hours.

5. Generously butter an 8-inch round cake tin.

6. Tip the dough out onto a lightly floured surface and knead gently to knock the air out. Using a lightly floured rolling pin, roll the dough out to a 9-by-12-inch rectangle. Brush the melted butter evenly over the surface of the dough. Sprinkle the brown sugar and dried fruits and peel evenly over the top, leaving about ⅓ inch free all the way around the rectangle.

7. Working from one long edge, roll the dough up tightly as if you were making a jelly roll. Brush the other long edge of the dough with water and seal carefully, pinching it shut. Cut the roll crosswise into 9 equal pieces. Place the rolls, cut-side up, in the prepared cake tin, placing one roll in the center and the remaining 8 around the outside. Cover the tin with oiled plastic wrap and set aside in a warm place for another 30 minutes to rest and rise again.

8. Preheat the oven to 375°F/190°C.

9. Bake for 30 to 35 minutes, until risen and golden brown. Remove from the oven and carefully tip the buns out onto a wire rack, right-side up.

10. Brush the honey over the tops of the buns while still warm. Pull apart and serve warm, with or without butter for spreading.

Iced Buns

Soft and yeasty with a delicious icing glaze and glacé cherry topping, these delicious buns were made famous in the 2003 British comedy film *Calendar Girls*. Children everywhere, both old and young, love them. *Makes 8*

PREP TIME: 20 minutes, plus 1 hour 45 minutes to rise **BAKE TIME:** 10 minutes

1½ tablespoons butter
⅓ cup (80 mL) water
Scant ⅓ cup (70 mL)
  whole milk
2 tablespoons fine granu-
  lated sugar (caster sugar)

1¾ cups (250 grams)
  strong bread flour, plus
  more for dusting
2¼ teaspoons
  fast-acting yeast
1 teaspoon fine sea salt

1 medium free-range egg
½ cup (65 grams) icing
  (confectioners')
  sugar, sifted
1 tablespoon water
4 glacé cherries, halved

1. Combine the butter, water, milk, and sugar in a saucepan. Warm the mixture over low heat until lukewarm. It should not be hot to the touch. If it is too hot, you will kill the yeast. If you think it is too hot, let it cool to lukewarm.

2. Combine the flour and yeast in the bowl of a stand mixer fitted with a dough hook. Add the salt around the edges of the bowl. Pour in the milk mixture and the egg. Mix together on low for 4 to 5 minutes to combine all the ingredients. Increase the speed to medium and mix for an additional 6 minutes, until smooth and satiny.

3. Scrape out the dough onto a lightly floured surface and knead for a few minutes. Transfer to a lightly oiled bowl. Cover with lightly oiled plastic wrap and set aside in a warm place to rise for 1 hour. The dough should double in size. (Alternatively, you can do this with an electric hand mixer, but it will take you a bit longer to get a smooth satin-textured dough.)

4. Lightly grease a rimmed baking sheet.

5. Divide the dough into 8 equal pieces. (You can weigh the full dough on a scale, then divide by 8. Each portion should weigh the same amount.) Shape each piece into a round bun, then place them on the prepared baking sheet, seam-side down, leaving plenty of space in between each. Cover lightly with oiled plastic wrap and set aside in a warm place to rise for an additional 45 minutes. Again, they should double in size.

6. Preheat the oven to 425°F/220°C.

7. Bake for 7 to 8 minutes, until light golden brown and fluffy. They should be golden brown on the undersides also, and sound hollow when tapped on the underside. Transfer to a wire rack to cool completely.

8. Once completely cooled, whisk the icing sugar together with just enough water to give you a nice thick and sticky glaze icing. Dip the tops of the cooled buns into this icing, pop them back onto the baking tray, icing-side up, and place half a glacé cherry in the middle of each. Leave to set before serving. These are best eaten the same day.

Technique Tip: For optimum flavor, don't glaze and decorate until you are ready to serve!

Hot Cross Buns

These spiced and fruity buns are an Easter tradition all over the UK, though they are available in the shops all year round now. Nothing beats the delicious flavor of a freshly baked hot cross bun, split, toasted, and spread with butter. These buns normally have a pastry cross baked into the top, but it is also quite acceptable to cut a cross on top if you prefer. They are glazed after baking with a water-sugar glaze. You can also pipe a cross on top with a thick glacé icing after they cool (see tip). *Makes 1 dozen*

PREP TIME: 30 minutes, plus 2 hours to rise **BAKE TIME:** 15 minutes

For the buns

3¼ cups (450 grams) strong white bread flour, plus more for dusting

¼ cup (50 grams) fine granulated sugar (caster sugar)

2¼ teaspoons fast-acting yeast

1 teaspoon salt

1 teaspoon mixed spice (see page 8)

1 teaspoon ground cinnamon

½ teaspoon freshly grated nutmeg

3½ tablespoons butter, melted and cooled

⅔ cup (160 mL) luke-warm milk

¼ cup (60 mL) luke-warm water

1 large free-range egg, lightly beaten

½ cup (75 grams) dried currants

⅓ cup (50 grams) chopped candied peel

For the pastry crosses (optional)

⅓ cup (50 grams) plain all-purpose flour

2 tablespoons butter

Water as needed

For the glaze

2 tablespoons water

2 tablespoons granulated sugar

1. Combine the flour, sugar, yeast, salt, mixed spice, cinnamon, and nutmeg in a large bowl. Mix them completely. In a measuring cup with a spout, whisk together the melted and cooled butter, milk, water, and egg. Make a well in the center of the dry ingredients and pour in the wet, then add the currants and candied peel on top.

2. Mix with a wooden spoon to form a soft dough. Tip the dough out onto a lightly floured surface. Knead by hand for about 10 minutes until you have a smooth and elastic dough. Shape the dough into a smooth ball. Add the ball of dough to an oiled

bowl, turning to coat it with oil. Cover with oiled plastic wrap and set aside in a warm place to rise until doubled in size, about 1½ hours.

3. Butter 2 rimmed baking sheets.

4. Tip the risen dough out onto a lightly floured surface and knead it gently for 2 to 3 minutes. Divide the dough into 12 equal pieces. (You can weigh the dough on a scale and then divide it by 12. This is the weight each piece of dough should be.) Shape each piece into a round, poking any currants or peel that pop out back into the dough.

5. Place the buns spaced well apart on the prepared baking sheets. Flatten them slightly with the palm of your hand and cut a cross into the top of each one with a sharp knife. Cover lightly with greased plastic wrap and set aside to rise in a warm place until doubled in size, about 30 minutes.

6. Preheat the oven to 425°F/220°C.

7. While the buns are rising, you can make the pastry crosses, if you like. Put the flour in a small bowl and rub in the butter. Add only enough water to make a stiff dough, then roll out onto a lightly floured surface using a floured rolling pin. Cut into thin strips, no more than ⅓ inch wide. Moisten one side of the pastry strips and lay in a cross pattern over the top of each bun.

8. Bake the buns for 15 minutes, until golden brown. They should sound hollow when tapped on the bottoms when done. While the buns are baking, prepare the sugar glaze by gently heating the water and sugar together until the sugar dissolves. Brush this mixture over the hot buns as soon as they come out of the oven.

Variation Tip: To make a glacé icing to pipe crosses on top, whisk together ½ cup (65 grams) icing (confectioners') sugar and just enough cold water to make a thick glaze. Pop this into a small resealable plastic bag. Cut a small part from one corner of the baggie and use this to pipe crosses onto the tops of the completely cooled buns.

Old-Fashioned Hovis Loaf

This is a much-beloved whole-wheat bread in the UK. Typically, it is baked using strong white bread flour with the addition of wheat germ. A bit of dark treacle is added for sweetness, which also serves to give it a lovely brown color. There is an iconic advertisement for the store brand that shows a young boy walking his push bike up a steep cobbled street, a loaf of fresh Hovis bread in his basket. This vision never fails to tug on the heartstrings and make one long for an older, simpler time. *Makes 1 loaf*

PREP TIME: 30 minutes, plus 2 hours to rise BAKE TIME: 30 minutes

Scant 1¼ cups (280 mL) lukewarm water

1 tablespoon dark treacle or blackstrap molasses

1½ teaspoons regular dried yeast

3⅔ cups (500 grams) strong bread flour, plus more for dusting

7 tablespoons (110 grams) wheat germ

1½ teaspoons salt

1 tablespoon canola oil

1. Combine the lukewarm water and treacle in a large measuring cup and stir to dissolve. Add the yeast and stir. Leave to proof for 10 minutes. The mixture should look nice and bubbly and have a definite yeasty fragrance.

2. Whisk the flour, wheat germ, and salt together in a bowl. Add the yeast mixture along with the oil and stir everything together into a soft dough. It should be a bit tacky.

3. Tip the dough out onto a lightly floured surface. Knead well for about 10 minutes, until you have a smooth, satiny elastic dough, adding flour as needed to keep the dough from sticking. Shape into a ball and place in a lightly oiled bowl, turning to coat the top with oil. Cover with oiled plastic wrap and place in a warm place to rise until doubled in size, about 1 hour.

4. Generously butter an 8-by-4-inch loaf tin and set aside.

5. Tip the risen dough out onto a lightly floured surface and knead gently for 2 to 3 minutes to knock out any air. Shape the dough into a loaf and smooth the top and ends. Place in the prepared loaf tin. Cover loosely with lightly oiled plastic wrap and place in a warm place for an additional hour to rise. At the end of that time, it should almost fill the pan.

6. Preheat the oven to 375°F/190°C.

7. Bake for 30 to 35 minutes, until well risen and nicely browned. When done, the loaf should sound hollow on the bottom when lightly tapped. Tip the loaf out onto a wire rack and cool completely.

Crumpets

Crumpets are small, round yeasted breads cooked on a griddle pan. Soft and spongy and filled with lovely holes, these are perfect for holding all that butter and jam spread on top. These are the perfect addition to a tea party! You will need 4-inch metal cooking rings to cook these. *Makes 8*

PREP TIME: 15 minutes, plus 1 hour to rise **BAKE TIME:** 10 minutes

1⅓ cups plus 1 tablespoon (330 mL) whole milk

1 teaspoon fine granulated sugar (caster sugar)

1⅔ cups (225 grams) all-purpose flour

1 teaspoon fine sea salt

2¼ teaspoons fast-acting yeast

Canola oil, for greasing

1. Put the milk and sugar in a saucepan and heat gently over medium-low heat to dissolve the sugar. The milk should not be hot; it should only be lukewarm. If it gets too hot, allow it to cool to lukewarm. Remove the pan from the heat and pour the milk into a large measuring cup with a pouring spout.

2. Sift the flour into a bowl and whisk in the salt and yeast. Make a well in the center. Pour in the lukewarm milk and whisk both together until you have a smooth, lump-free batter. Cover with a clean tea towel and set aside in a warm place to rise for 1 hour.

3. When you are ready to cook the crumpets, preheat the oven to 250°F/125°C. Heat a tiny bit of oil in a large heavy-bottomed nonstick skillet over low heat. Generously coat four 4-inch cooking rings with oil. Place them in the skillet. Spoon a heaping tablespoon of crumpet batter into each ring.

4. Cook for 3 to 4 minutes, until the surface of the crumpets are covered with tiny air bubbles. Once the bubbles begin to pop, remove the rings and carefully turn the crumpets over. The crumpets should be golden brown on the underside. Cook for 1 minute longer.

5. Keep the crumpets warm in the oven while you cook the remainder of the crumpets, re-oiling the rings and the pan.

Measurement Conversions

	US STANDARD	US STANDARD (OUNCES)	METRIC (APPROXIMATE)
VOLUME EQUIVALENTS (LIQUID)	2 tablespoons	1 fl. oz.	30 mL
	¼ cup	2 fl. oz.	60 mL
	½ cup	4 fl. oz.	120 mL
	1 cup	8 fl. oz.	240 mL
	1½ cups	12 fl. oz.	355 mL
	2 cups or 1 pint	16 fl. oz.	475 mL
	4 cups or 1 quart	32 fl. oz.	1 L
	1 gallon	128 fl. oz.	4 L
VOLUME EQUIVALENTS (DRY)	⅛ teaspoon	————	0.5 mL
	¼ teaspoon	————	1 mL
	½ teaspoon	————	2 mL
	¾ teaspoon	————	4 mL
	1 teaspoon	————	5 mL
	1 tablespoon	————	15 mL
	¼ cup	————	59 mL
	⅓ cup	————	79 mL
	½ cup	————	118 mL
	⅔ cup	————	156 mL
	¾ cup	————	177 mL
	1 cup	————	235 mL
	2 cups or 1 pint	————	475 mL
	3 cups	————	700 mL
	4 cups or 1 quart	————	1 L
	½ gallon	————	2 L
	1 gallon	————	4 L
WEIGHT EQUIVALENTS	½ ounce	————	15 g
	1 ounce	————	30 g
	2 ounces	————	60 g
	4 ounces	————	115 g
	8 ounces	————	225 g
	12 ounces	————	340 g
	16 ounces or 1 pound	————	455 g

	FAHRENHEIT (F)	CELSIUS (C) (APPROXIMATE)
OVEN TEMPERATURES	250°F	120°C
	300°F	150°C
	325°F	180°C
	375°F	190°C
	400°F	200°C
	425°F	220°C
	450°F	230°C

Resources

BOOKS

Mary Berry's Ultimate Cake Book, Mary Berry, 1994, BBC Books

This was one of the first books I purchased when I moved to the UK in 2000 and has been an invaluable resource for great classic recipes for cakes, biscuits, traybakes, scones, and more. I highly recommend.

Delia Smith's Complete Cookery Course, Delia Smith, 1992, BBC Books

I received this book for Christmas from my husband in 2003. It is a wonderful resource for how to cook British, from soup to nuts and everything in between. It has excellent conversion tables as well.

New British Classics, Gary Rhodes, 1999, BBC Books

This was the first cookbook I purchased when I moved to the UK in 2000. It, too, has been invaluable in my journey toward becoming an accomplished British cook and baker. It features good, solid recipes of the old favorites with a modern twist.

Be-Ro Home Baked Recipes, Be-Ro Flour

This is a great basic baking book, covering scones, biscuits, cakes, pastry, pies, and all things in between. If you can get your hands on one of these, you have a treasure. Mine was a gift from a friend.

SHOPPING

Amazon has everything you need as far as baking-related materials and ingredients are concerned and is an invaluable resource for baking pans and British ingredients.

Amazon.com

British Food Shop is a great source of British ingredients. It carries everything from jams to spreads to essential baking ingredients, including suet, dark treacle, a variety of sugars and flours, and preserved ginger in syrup.

BritishFoodShop.com

British Corner Shop is also a great resource for British ingredients, carrying a wide variety of British goods and ingredients.

BritishCornerShop.co.uk

Index

Acknowledgments

To Callisto Media and Anne Lowrey, thank you so very much for affording me the opportunity to share my love of British baking with the world.

To my mother, and her mother, and her mother before her, generations of good cooks who fed their families well and who inspired me to want to do the same.

To my children, who were my guinea pigs throughout the years and upon whom I cut my culinary teeth.

To my father, sister, and brother who have always been my biggest fans, but especially to my father and mother, who gave me wings and encouraged me to use them. Family—it's not a small thing. It's everything.

About the Author

 **Marie Rayner** is a retired professional chef, food blogger, and cookbook author. She began her culinary career working as a pastry chef at a hotel back in the 1970s, then took time off to raise a family. In 2000 she moved to the UK, where she worked as a personal chef for several years before retiring from the trade several years ago. In 2009 she started the award-winning food blog The English Kitchen (TheEnglishKitchen.co), where she shares her lifetime of cooking experience with tried-and-true recipes, along with many beloved and traditional British recipes. She does all the testing, so you don't have to. Marie is the author of several cookbooks, including *Recipes from the Big Blue Binder* and *The English Kitchen: An Anglophile's Love Note to English Cuisine*. She created an award-winning recipe for the British Turkey Federation in 2012, which went on to win a prestigious Turkey Award at the national level. She and her blog have been highlighted in *The Times* of London and the Canadian *HELLO!* magazine. Her motto is "Food doesn't have to be complicated to be delicious."

CPSIA information can be obtained
at www.ICGtesting.com
Printed in the USA
BVHW062241030122
625372BV00001B/1